JARED NEWSON

30 MINUTES

THAT CAN CHANGE YOUR LIFE

A DAILY ROUTINE FOR LETTING GO OF YOUR EGO AND
ALLOWING THE GREATNESS WITHIN TO SHINE BRIGHT

GRINDLOUD
Grindloud Consulting
11807 Allisonville Rd. STE 570
Fishers, IN 46038
www.newaynation.com

*"When your motivation and desire is
to help other people win,
how can you lose?"*

-Jared Newson

Published in Fishers, Indiana by Grindloud Consulting, LLC.

Contact the author at jared@newaynation.com for information about special discounts for bulk purchases, sales promotions, fund-raising, and educational needs.

ISBN 978-1736932209 (Paperback)
ISBN 978-1736932216 (eBook)

Grindloud Consulting
11807 Allisonville Rd. STE 570
Fishers, IN 46038
www.newaynation.com

Praise for *30 Minutes That Can Change Your Life*

"The tone and tenor of the chapters included were both inspiring and applicable to people of all ages and backgrounds. They were grounded in biblical principles and will resonate with anyone who wants to be better. Michele and I found ourselves drawing off our own backgrounds, be it athletically (a very long time ago), professionally and as parents.

You attacked things head-on and got straight to the point, something that is woefully missing in today's society. The way you correlated the power that the mind and the devil have to influence not just how we feel, but what we believe was very powerful. I couldn't help but think about today's youth and all the outlets that are out there for them to feel that they are not enough.

I believe this book will positively impact anyone who takes the time to read it and follow your advice.

We truly feel blessed to have crossed paths. I hope this book impacts the lives of many."

- Josh & Michelle Cooper

"I enjoyed reading and it stimulated thought of how I can do better living in the now. That's a good thing and will help people. I can say that I see the first chapter in action in your life. That makes it real and honest.

The reference I AM is a strong meaning in many ways to a lot of differing audiences perceiving it in many different ways.

King David said, 'It is better to not say than to have to unsay.' We can all learn from that. It is best to be slow to action so that we do not have to undo the action as some can not be undone.

I think your book will be awesome. It is a wise man that seeks counsel but it is a Godly man that obeys the Lord. The two will not always match as God tests who you will listen to."

- Greg Lymberopolous

"I was moved by your presentation. That first chapter was inspiring and engaging and your literary transitions kept me moving to the next paragraph to see what the next concept would be.

I pray you'll continue to let the Lord guide you as you share with the world the wisdom of your life experiences."

- TD Robinson

"So much of what you wrote about resonates not only with me but I am sure the younger generation as well. I wish I knew and understood your theory and meaning behind 'I AM' years ago! I need to appreciate the memories and the journey. The biggest take away I got was forgiving people with egos and to 'understand that evolution has not yet become a part of their lives.' Very insightful and very well written, my friend. As always, you will continue to impact many people from your experiences! There is a lot of great information in your book that these kids need to hear!!"

- Julie Mccomb

"I have read it many times hoping I could find something to contribute positive changes & truly would not change anything. When reading it I thought of if I had read this as a teenager, a newly married woman, a young mother, a newly divorced woman & the many other stages of my life, what would I have taken away? Let's just say it would have helped me in every stage. Congrats on what you have created & how you are using your God given gifts & talents to help others."

- Laura Shonk

"I AM."

- Jeff Becker

"Chapter one really resonates with a lot of things I have been learning and putting into practice in my own life over the last year or so!

This line especially resonated, 'Let's get something straight: being aware of your ego does not tell you who you are. Being aware of your ego tells you who you are not.'

Through reading up on a spiritual personality framework called the Enneagram, that perspective of the ego has been key for me.

You are speaking a lot of mindfulness as well, even some breath work with the one breath and I AM affirmation. I love it!"

- Ariela Mckenzie

"We discussed and talked about it and it is so crazy how it aligns with our life, our mission, our future right now. The pandemic year truly set us on a new and bigger path. Chapter one has us ready to read the rest of the book. We are excited for you and excited for the world to read these words."

- Trudy Henderson and Chris Brinkley

CONTENTS

PREFACE

Welcome to *30 Minutes That Can Change Your Life*. I came up with this title in 2015 while living in Orchies, France. At that time, I only had the title and chapters of the book in mind but I knew it was the start of something I wanted to share with others. I have always been a person drawn to self-motivation. Anything motivational, growth, or development related, I was in on it. I've had the desire to put together a book of substance ever since developing the idea in France. Fast forward a few years to May 2020 in Fishers, Indiana, when I decided to open my old notes and begin writing. This book is a collection of motivational topics, lectures, books, trials and tribulations, and experiences from throughout this life I live.

My goal for writing this is to be able to reach just one individual in a positive way. That is one of my daily mantras: to impact just one person. That one person on whom you have an effect will reach someone else and from there, it's a domino effect. *30 Minutes That Can Change Your Life* is a book that has enough substance to guide you along your journey yet is short enough for you to approach without feeling like it's a real time commitment. It was important to me to write a book that was approachable for everyone regardless of background. Each chapter has an affirmation to speak before reading. This affirmation carries throughout as a theme for each chapter. I love affirmations because it speaks power within yourself when you chant them. It's almost like opening your mind and your heart to receive each chapter in a mindful way. I live the values and mantras I write about here, and do believe that this book will allow you to see things through a different lens. Change is necessary and growth is mandatory.

Who doesn't have 30 minutes to better themselves each day? Though you may not be able to read the book in entirety in 30 minutes, you can apply these chapters 30 minutes per day throughout your life. I do pray that you receive the love that I've poured into these chapters in a blessed way and that I can become an inspiration to you to give the same love to all of mankind. Here's to *30 Minutes That Can Change Your Life*.

CHAPTER 1:
LET GO "EGO"

AFFIRMATION:

Today and every day
moving forward,
I understand that "I am."

What is an ego? WordNet dictionary defines an ego as "an inflated feeling of pride in your superiority to others." I will tell you this: there is no way that you can battle against it and come out victorious. Becoming an amazing person does not happen by simply trying to be an amazing person. You become amazing by finding the light that is already in you and letting that light shine. The only way to make that light shine its brightest is by evolving mentally and allowing yourself to move past your ego.

The word "I" is the biggest mistake, as well as the greatest fact. Let me explain. What do you think goes through the mind of a person on their death-bed? They realize that the only thing that matters is the present moment, and nothing material ever had any real attachment to them. They realize that the life they lived was actually a blessing and what they spent their life searching for was deep inside of them the entire time. They appreciate the memories and the journey. This realization would not have arisen if they were not forced to minimize their ego. In the regular, day to day moments, what do you think the ego would have done? Do you think it would have held on to old grudges or worried about the latest sneakers coming out? The ego causes you to have attachment to things, as well as an attachment with your mind. **YOU ARE NOT YOUR MIND.**

Are you an energy person? Do you feed off the energy currents of others? If the answer is yes, then this is a form of the ego. How often are you lost in your thoughts and wrapped up in the voice in your head?

Let's go back to the person near death. When things that you thought you had an attachment to, things that you thought gave you life, things that you thought made you whole are all taken away, who are you? When you have nothing else to identify with, WHO ARE YOU? Why would you wait until your dying days to realize or find out who you are? Here's a fun fact: I am not a writer. I am not a mentor. I AM. The affirmation of this chapter is, "Today and every day moving forward, I understand that I AM." In this chapter, you will learn the meaning of I AM.

YOU MUST FIRST SEE VALUE IN YOURSELF IN ORDER TO ADD VALUE TO YOURSELF.

You can see the pimple on your sister's back, but cannot see the cyst on your own. What does that mean? It means when you judge the next person, it makes you feel bigger. It boosts your ego. It enlarges you. Your ego needs fuel to keep going. Complaining, slandering, telling false information to start gossip, jealousy, and bullying are all part of the ego. What is complaining, exactly? It's made-up stories that your ego wants you to believe to be the truth. We all know someone who is always complaining and has an excuse for everything. These complaints and excuses are actually ego boosts in disguise. They know if they complain, they will have an audience. The ego loves a crowd of believers and cheerleaders. A bunch of like-minded complainers. Oh, how big will that ego be after getting others to feed into your own agenda? Real big.

In my journey of living, I had to come to understand that things are not always personal. It took me quite a bit of time to realize this. I had a quick trigger, protecting myself as if I was always being disrespected. I had to react every time. But reacting every time put me at the mercy of whomever interacted with me. Once I realized not to take anything personally, I stopped reacting. However, when an egotistical person sees that you will not feed into their mind games, you better be ready for the war games. This is the only way for them to feel dominant or superior. So be aware of the many tricks they will try to play in order to gain an edge on you. Understand that they are who they are and it has nothing to do with you. Forgive them. Understand that evolution has not yet become a part of their lives. They are simply unaware.

The times when I took everything personally were the times when my ego was big. I had SUCH a big ego. I was quick to generalize or categorize a person just because of something they may have said that rubbed my ego the wrong way. I was blinded. I saw the words and how they sculpted my thoughts, but I didn't see who the person was inside. I lost many connections and potential friendships in my big ego days because I refused to make amends even if I realized I was wrong. My ego took over and became stronger. I didn't see them as an individual. I

SAW THEM AS A THREAT.

I have a friend that is always annoyed by something. Always. There's something wrong with anything and everything in life. Not enough ice in the water glass, the food is warm but not hot, the food is too hot now, this lady keeps looking at me the wrong way, etc. You get where I am going. It's an addiction. Sounds weird right? They are addicted to being annoyed. It gives them life. The ego becomes stronger. Be wary of the person who's always right. You may catch yourself saying: Dude, if you know everything, then why the hell are you still in this space at this particular time? That person, no matter the real factual answer, will always have the correct one.

IT'S AN AMAZING FEELING WHEN YOU DISSOCIATE YOURSELF FROM YOUR EGO.

How do I do this? Understand it for what it is: your mind. Once it loses its control over you, you can see individuals for who they are. Nobody is wrong. Forgiveness is forgiveness but let's not be stupid. Some individuals are so deep into their ego that they refuse the change or look into themselves. Being nonreactive to a person and understanding that they are just unaware doesn't mean you shouldn't remain conscious of danger or protect yourself if you feel threatened. Being conscious of your ego can only be felt in the present. Take a deep breath for a second. Focus on that breath and that breath alone. Remove any thoughts in your mind. Do you feel present at that particular moment? **I AM.**

Have you ever felt the need to be in control of a situation or to seek attention from someone else? Of course. The hidden agenda is present. You need that situation or person to succeed in strengthening your ego. But what happens next?

You will need that next situation to happen soon because you are never satisfied. Fear is the cause of your hidden agenda. Fear of not being enough, not succeeding, not being seen. In the sports world, as well as the world in general, mentioning a person you are associated with as a higher power is an ego boost. You might know it as name dropping. "Do you know such and such? That's my boy." You are trying to gain respect or a sense of appreciation for being tied to someone of importance. Being cool by association.

It's always good to reset. The attention seeking ego plays a role in order to get its fix. Could be from material satisfaction, some type of gratification, or even superiority. Why would your ego play a role? It's simple. The ego is never satisfied. It believes, "I am not good enough." The thought of you needing to get more so that you can be more is false. Why? Because you are already one with life. In the physical world, we do have classifications. Some people are in positions of power that make them superior, according to social norms. What if I told you that we are neither inferior nor superior to anyone? The ego creates the separation and heartache. **I AM.**

Not getting enough praise from your spouse? Recognition at work? Everyone sleeping on you? All questions for which your ego is looking to find answers. Temper tantrums, having negative reactions just to draw attention – these are all the ego's doing. In my opinion, one of the most comical forms of ego is playing the victim. I get a deep internal chuckle when I see this. (The exterior is stoic but the internal is a two-year-old being tickled. Non-stop laughter.)

The victim seeker, or as we call them, "woe is me." They will search for pity in all forms, sympathy, and anyone willing to listen to their story. In their eyes, they have been misjudged, misguided, misunderstood, and disrespected. They have become the victim. There's no turning back. This is what they associate as and how they see themselves. The past ego in me would want to tell them to shut up and stop whining. The large part of me understands what they are. I understand what is. **I AM.**

I always try to help people in these situations. Words of encouragement, personal testimonies and such are examples that could lead to the "victim seeker" looking at themselves from within instead of from the exterior. Or maybe not. It's easy to become engulfed in feeling guilty for a person such as this. Your own personal ego will be tested in all circumstances. Don't fall into old habits.

TAKE A DEEP BREATH. FOCUS ON THAT BREATH AND THAT BREATH ALONE. COME BACK TO THE PRESENT.

We all know the saying, "I'm living my best life." What does that really mean? Are you truly living your best life? You do not actually live your life, life lives you. Are you a roller coaster of emotions? Check this out: you do not have to be. Be aware of your thoughts and emotions when they arise, consciously making a change from thinking to being aware. That little voice in your head does have a life and mind of its own. Some people are prisoners to that voice. You may be on a great path and then...boom. That voice brings up a past event that triggers you. You quickly respond and react. One point for the ego, zero points for being in the now.

YOU ARE NOT YOUR MIND. The voice in

your head pretends to be you, but it is not. That voice tells the body something and the body reacts. Emotions pour out and now you feed those thoughts your attention. I'll give you an example. A father is in the park with his toddler. Another man walks past the park and says to the guy, "What brought you here today?" Seems like an innocent conversation starter, but before you know it, boom. The guy is punched in the nose. In the father's eyes, this other gentleman was judging and questioning his presence at that park. His mind was triggered by a past situation of anger and he went immediately into defense mode. With everything going on in the world today, everyone is on edge. Small words can become big problems. Thoughts that trigger emotion in the body happen so fast, the body reacts before you may have time to assess. This is why emotions of the past that were traumatic need to be attended to, not swept under the rug. Negative emotions come back to haunt you.

So the question is **WHO ARE YOU?** If I had to answer this question years ago, I would have said, "My name is Jared Newson. A professional basketball player and trainer. I am a son, a brother, and a believer. A focused individual with the need to motivate and inspire others. A person who believes in love and forgiveness." There's more, but I will stop there. These things were what mattered to me in life.

Because of this, they also had the power to piss me off and disrupt my energy. If I had a bad game, I was upset for the whole day. Everyone would be affected by my attitude. If I didn't get the ball for several possessions, the whole team and the coach was going to hear about it. If my mother said something that she knew would trigger me, well, I was going to be triggered. I was small-minded. Small situations got to me.

So what's the answer to "Who are you?" For me back then, it would have been, "I am small." What are things that really matter to you? Be honest with yourself. The most dishonest thing you can do to yourself is lie. The world will show you what really matters to you. You can read a self-help book, or maybe this book will be one to help you on your journey.

Three months pass and you say, "Nothing can get to me. I don't take anything personally." Your way of dealing with situations is ignoring and avoiding them. You are doing yourself a disservice. Once faced head-on with these issues that were overlooked, how are you going to react? This is the test. Take yourself and your ego out of the equation. Look at the person from within and not the ego in them. Looking at the ego in them strengthens the ego in you. You become petty and vindictive all over again.

NO ONE CAN TELL YOU WHO YOU ARE. YOU DO NOT NEED TO BELIEVE YOU ARE A CERTAIN PERSON. YOU SIMPLY ARE. I AM.

Have you ever complained to your spouse about not being communicative enough or not giving enough physical touch? Have you then looked at yourself and noticed that you are reacting to your spouse because it's actually inside of you that you see? You criticize someone else for something that you want, but do not give. Your ego is at full strength. So now, you choose to consciously refrain from communication and physical touch because you believe your spouse is purposely doing this in return. It's a war with your mind. You are fighting your own ego and losing. You have become the victim. Let's get something straight: being aware of your ego does not tell you who you are. Being aware of your ego tells you who you are not. You are not your mind. If you think the world owes you love, give the world love. If you think the world owes you respect, give respect. How can you receive anything that you do not give? Here's the kicker: you already have inside of you what you think you do not have. You've put a lid on the abundance cup that you are not allowing to be poured.

Have you ever visited a place like Jamaica? You will find that they are some of the most joyous people you will ever meet. Some don't appear to have ownership of anything, but they feel full. They let life live within them. A touchy subject in the world today is religion. Different beliefs, different teachings, and several contradictions. Growing up in a certain religion may cause you not to fully find out who YOU are because of what you are taught to believe.

You are fearful to find out about yourself because you are afraid that you will find out that you do not align with the teachings you grew up on. What would you find out? Nothing. It is said that knowing yourself is actually being yourself, not what someone else wants you to be. "Living my best life" is not that at all. This is a reference of living the life that you seem to have. You are identifying yourself with what the world deems as good or bad, happy or unhappy.

Living in the now is no easy task. There is always a task at hand. This statement is part of the issue. If you look at the living in the now as a task, it will indeed be a task. There will be no end and you will search for the next issue to pop up. Life is now. You only have this moment. Think about it: how does the past come about? Because it's a thought in your mind. How does the future come about? Because it's a thought in your mind.

CHAPTER 2:
LEAD ME TO THE
WATER

AFFIRMATION:

If I can make just one person's life better,
the life I live will have
much more significance.

Are you a leader? Leaders are those who have positive intentions on those that they lead. Teaching, building character, and caring are all aspects of leadership. Being a leader is not by mistake. Leaders are often viewed as being role models as well. Of course, there are positive and negative role models, but the leaders with the primary focus on inspiring and encouraging others are the ones that I am talking about. When you choose a role model or leader to follow, which characteristics drew you to them? Was it because they were rich? Was it because they won a lot of championships? Was it because they were popular and deemed successful? Now, look at the person who's a mentor to you. Take away the accolades, the money, the popularity. Will this person still be a leader or role model in your mind? If the answer is no, then you should search for different criteria. How does that person affect the people around them? Now, ask yourself the same question. What type of effect do you have on the people around you? Without having to give deep thought on the question, do you help to bring out the strengths in others and not the weaknesses? When was the last time you made a teammate better off the field? When was the last time you made your family or peers better? What I mean by "better" is by sincerely and genuinely caring for their personal development with no ulterior motive or need for acknowledgment.

Leaders measure their success differently. Empowering another person is deemed successful to a leader. Building those relationships in order to shape and mold other potential leaders. For me, it's about giving back. The leadership I lacked in my life as a kid in sports, I gained during my adulthood with books and individuals God placed my life. As a teenager, I was the man of my family. The one who was expected to make it out and reach places no one had reached before. The problem with having that weight on your shoulders is that unless the ones counting on you are nurturing you for the better, there will be conflict in the end. True agendas became present as I continued on my path of growth. If a person sees that you are not genuine, you will not be trusted to lead or give any advice. Simple facts. Leadership can be deemed difficult if you in fact view it as a task. Leadership is basically influence. Whatever type of influence you give off to another person, you are leading. The question is, are you a positive or negative influence?

LEADERS MEASURE THEIR SUCCESS DIFFERENTLY.

I manage a fitness facility. But this alone does not make me a leader. On the exterior I display leadership because the staff must comply with the rules and regulations, but title does not necessarily permit leadership. My true leadership comes from intentionally caring for each and every one of the staff members or the organization's well-being. Encouraging them to achieve their fitness goals, empowering them to help grow the organization, and understanding that family comes first with their work schedules. Getting in the trenches to help scrub floors with the maintenance staff or scrubbing toilets. True leaders have to show that they are willing to put in the work as well.

Lead for the benefit of others, not for individual accolades. How great of a feeling is it when someone over whom you had a significance influence achieves great feats? You always have the opportunity to plant seeds of success. Whatever setting you are in, you can develop yourself into a leader. Not voicing that you are the leader, but influencing those around you in a positive manner. Investing time, energy and wisdom into the improvement of people around you.

LEAD FOR THE BENEFIT OF OTHERS, NOT FOR INDIVIDUAL ACCOLADES.

Think about the people who have touched you in a positive way. A parent, a coach, teacher, even a friend of a friend. While attending college at The University of Tennessee at Martin, I had the niche of being a self-made basketball player coming up. I used to embrace this title, but in fact I was not a self-made player, as much as I don't want to admit it. Yes, I put in the work with no one having to tell me, and yes, I did a lot of training and studying on my own. But just because I did not have a person with me physically does not mean I did not have a person with me spiritually. God has always been with me. My mother has always been there as a motivation. Rest in peace to my ex-coach Earl Holloway, who was there all the time calling to check on me every step of the way. I had a coach by the name of Jason James while in college. He is what I consider a leader because he was willing to get in the trenches when asked, and still to this day needed no acknowledgment to why and what he was doing for me.

6:00 am workouts on a continual basis before school, he was there to open the gym. Phone calls to talk out my frustrations, he was there to answer the phone. People along the way like Coach James are the reason I do what I do now. I have helped mentor a lot of athletes, friends, and family members. I've helped negotiate contracts for players, and didn't need any compensation from it. I never once asked them to give me a shoutout or tell people what I did. There are plenty of these people I've mentored who've made it to millionaire status and all I've ever wished for them is to continue to inspire others during their journey. If they never mention my name, I would still be at peace. They know as well as I do who was there for them.

Why? Because I don't care. My intentions are for them to succeed. I wholeheartedly am not a mentor because of the money. I want to see each person I have a relationship with find their purpose, live it out, and offer the favor to another. I believe the term now is "pay it forward." If you are a person like this, then that is awesome. Sometimes the results of your leadership may not always be apparent. It could take years and years down the line before someone recognizes that what you did for them resulted in how they approach life.

Having faith that no matter the outcome of your leadership, you did it because you sincerely and genuinely cared, is all a person can ask for. Do not be a know it all, because you don't know it all. You can easily rub someone the wrong way by acting as such. Do you talk the talk and walk the walk? Are you only doing what you are doing in order to gain clout?

Leaders know that they are leaders. In sports, a coach may name a person as captain, but that captain may not have the influence of the team. This influence may come from another player. A poor captain in this situation will recognize that he does not have any influence and then attempt to sabotage the team or the player of influence. I've seen this happen. It happened to me. I was on a team where the coach named another player as captain. Everyone else on the team followed me because of my work ethic and my desire to win. This did not rub the so-called captain the right way. He tried to snitch to the coach about everything I was doing off the court, he went back to tell the coach about our locker room talks, and he would not pass me the ball in the games on purpose.

At this moment in my life, I was not as level-headed or as conscious of my actions as I am now. I labeled him as a rat and I handled it how an immature kid would and punched him a few times in the locker room. The great thing about having a group of followers that believe in you is that my teammates had my back even though I initiated it. They told the coach that I was only defending myself. That alone was all the clarification I needed in order to feel like I was doing the right thing in leading my team, even if I wasn't the captain in title.

LEADERS KNOW THAT THEY ARE LEADERS.

Now, what would a great captain would have done in order to avoid a few knuckles to the face? A real leader in that situation would approach the player of influence and talk with him. Learn the things he's doing in order to gain respect of the team. Continue to empower this player of influence for the betterment of everyone. A true leader would be self-less and would not need to seek opportunities for improvement from others.

My teammates chose to follow me even in a situation of negativity. This meant the world to me. The captain still remained the captain, but he had no voice. Only a label. The team went on to be the best team in the league with me being the leading scorer but ultimately losing in the finals. Years later, I heard from a teammate and he told me how much he respected the way that I carried myself and my professionalism. He said that he has carried himself the same way over the years and is now a mentor to younger guys trying to make it. This is what it's all about. This is success to a true leader. If you can look beyond yourself, you can reach a lot of people.

THE DESTINATION IS IMPORTANT, BUT THE JOURNEY IS WHAT YOU NEED TO FOCUS ON.

All situations in leadership are not the same. Different scenarios require different approaches. The common denominator in all the situations is to understand that it's not about you. It's about them. Are you willing to help others achieve great things and not receive any credit? If credit is all that you are looking for, stop now. Of course it's great to be recognized for things you put a lot of effort into. That's different. But building other leaders is a journey. Embrace that journey. You will reach the destination. Don't be afraid to empower someone who may potentially overshadow you in the long run.

As a leader, you can share whatever vision you want, but that does not mean everyone will embrace that vision. People have little patience and want instant gratification now. A leader's job is to stay the course. Continue to remind everyone of the vision. Your job is to inspire when times get tough. Not everyone is equipped to last the long haul, but you should be. We all know that vision means nothing without action. Leaders must take action in order to reach that vision. Being stuck in that beginner stage of planning can be a downfall. Get the ball rolling and take action. As a leader, what are things that you value?

The values you believe in will reflect how you approach any situation. Values determine who you are and what is important to you. It will be hard for a leader that does not value building relationships to try and build one. It's contradictory. Values matter. You've got to take a hard look inside yourself and identify your motivations. What drives you? What are you naturally gifted at? What are things that tend to be more challenging for you? At this point, you can't lie to yourself.

This is a judgment-free assessment of YOU. Look deep. What pisses you off, what makes you go, what makes you happy, what makes you sad? Find out the situations or things in your life that can be negatively transferred to other individuals. If you know that certain instances trigger you in a non-appealing way, then address this before you project it externally on to others. We are not perfect as individuals. Perfection is impossible.

Some situations simply cannot be changed. It's not an excuse or a free pass to not try. Effort must be applied before accepting that things cannot be changed. Whole-hearted effort. If, after giving complete effort, the situations that you try to change seem as if they're impeding or slowing down your progress for the better, let it go. There's no need to struggle with it. If the situation is with another person and you have done everything in your power to try and help, let it go.

You know the saying, "Hurt people, hurt people." Forgiving is difficult. Forgiving yourself is even more difficult. How hard is it to put your pride to the side in order to forgive someone and then ask them for forgiveness? Not difficult at all if you take out your pride. **Just do it**. Without an attitude and without believing someone owes you something, forgive and ask for forgiveness. Be a leader. Reach the potential that God wants you to reach. If you as a leader do not believe in yourself, you will soon run into the wall of rejection. The "fake it till you make it" phase will dwindle and you will be exposed. Leaders often take on the toughest tasks to be there for everyone, as well as handling their own issues. A great leader knows how to handle his lows and maintain his highs. Once I was able to influence a family member and a peer into becoming a leader themselves, it became like a drug for me. A satisfaction drug. I was hooked. Reaching a family member that was much older than me with much more life experience taught me that age was not a factor and what was inside of me did not need to be bottled up.

I was an introverted shy kid. I'll handle my business, you handle yours, and let's see who wins at the end of the day. If you fail, too bad – should've done it my way. These were my teenage years. I stuck with what I knew and ran with it. If you were to ask the majority people who have known me since my middle school and high school days, they would say that I kept to myself, had a small group of people

I associated with, and worked hard. I did not let people in on what I was working on. These characteristics do not just up and leave during your life. They still stick with you, but with a higher understanding of people and relationships as I have become more open, more willing to help, and less worried about people's opinions and judgements. I care and am in no search for a reward. In writing this book, my goal was to reach one person. Just one. Years and years of reading and experience poured into these pages, and all I wish to do is reach one person. If that one person is you, thank you. You've helped me reach my goal of feeling empowered and empowering others. Facing your past is never an easy assignment. It is what helps to mold and sculpt you. Remember, you are trying to move toward a place where you are no longer held back from past painful traumas that weigh you down. Respect and appreciate the journey. Taking the fast track and cutting corners in order to get the instant gratification will become a habit. It will become what you are known for – cutting corners when things get difficult. Keep at it and persevere. God is here for you. Instead of spending so much attention on where you are weak, spend more time focusing on your strengths.

Build your inner circle with people who complement your weak points. Having a bunch of like-minded friends who are emotionally weak will only keep you there. It's like having crabs in a barrel. In order to grow, you need to recognize what your strengths and weaknesses are. If you know a leader who has no weaknesses, run away. He's not real. Even super heroes have weaknesses. I personally can respect someone who can say, "I don't know the answer." I used to tell a girl I dated in the past that she should be on jeopardy because she had the answer to any and every question. She definitely could've won us a lot of money. Of course she didn't really have the answers but you can understand how it would feel if the person that you are always around can answer anything thrown their way. You do not have all the answers. Nor should you want to. For example, I know that I am imperfect. I actually know nothing at all. I am present in this world and aim to make an impact in a positive way. I am committed to growth, committed to evolving. I surround myself with people who complement my strengths, as well as my weaknesses. This is the foundation to achieving great things.

Chapter 3:
The "It" Factor

AFFIRMATION:

Today, I will start.
I will simply put my feet
in the starting blocks and
start the race.

What is the "it" factor? Daily actions that you consistently undertake that will either keep you stagnant or enhance you. The "it" factor is what will enable you to manifest whatever you desire to have or create in your life, and ultimately create the life you want. If you want to know what separates successful people from one another, it's not only having an "it" factor, but also knowing how to use it. Success is easy. Yes, you heard that correctly. Success is easy if you are doing the simple things that lead to success. On the contrary, it's just as easy to neglect to do those simple steps. Successful business owners listen to motivational material. Non-business owners listen to motivational material as well. The difference is that they choose different motivational material to listen to. Same end result, different avenues. Let me give you an example. Lisa and Lindsey were two high school students in the same classroom. The teacher asks both of them to pick out two books or magazines and complete a vision board. Lindsey picks her books and magazines first and completes her vision board. Lisa then does the same. Lindsey's vision board has a fast car, big house, an attractive model with his shirt off, designer clothes, a group of girls partying, a famous supermodel with her salary underneath, and several quotes such as "YOLO," "I do me," "Trust no one," and "Haters will hate."

Lisa's vision board has a person playing chess, an airplane with a map of Europe on it, a picture of several self-development books, a married couple with kids in the background, and several words such as "faith," "God is great," "I am," "I can," and "10 steps to being successful." I will let you be the judge of which one of their vision boards will lead to success. We have all the tools we need within us in order to change our lives. The question is, are you willing to remain disciplined and do the simple things everyday consistently? If the answer is yes, then this is the chapter you will want to really focus in on. Remember, success is easy to achieve, but without action, it can be difficult.

SUCCESS IS EASY TO ACHIEVE BUT WITHOUT ACTION, IT CAN BE HARD.

Time to dive into the "it" factor. This process will not happen overnight. The simple steps of action that will enable future success will not feel as if they're having a huge impact at first. But they are indeed important. Let me make sure you understand this process. You will not see it immediate, but you will definitely see long-term success. When I train my clients on the basketball court, we have days where we focus on swishes only. A swish is a jump shot hitting nothing but net. I will set a particular number of made shots to complete and they must achieve that number. In the process of focusing on only swishes, they are unintentionally making several jump shots in a row. They are becoming better shooters by focusing only on this specific task. Now, if I were to say, "Ok, we are going to make six jump shots in row." Now they are focused on just making the jump shots and may not be able to complete the task of making swishes because I changed the criteria. Their focus went only to what I required.

What you do today and every day matters. The people that understand the decisions made every day, whether big or small, are successful people. They choose to do the simple little things that may seem like no big deal, over and over and over. The little things that no one will applaud or even notice. The little things that may seem stupid to others.

How many times can you count where you were in a low situation – whether mentally, physically, emotionally, or spiritually – and in time, you ended up finally coming out of that low place? What happened during that process? I'm sure you were in such a rut that you told yourself or someone close to you, "That's enough. Time to go. Time to get out of this path of failure and back on track." This is the point where you began to implement those daily routines. Once you started feeling better and seeing results, you then started to slide back down that failure pole. Then back up again and back down again. You found a way to survive. You were having a seesaw battle within yourself. Why? You simply stopped doing all the little necessary things that helped you get your feet out of the mud. You saw the light at the tunnel and said to yourself, "I made it." Instead of having this roller coaster of emotions, all you had to do was consistently complete the simple steps. That is the difference between people with the "it" factor and people without it. Discipline.

Writing down goals, meditating first thing in the morning when you wake up, praying, speaking only positive words out of your mouth. These may seem like simple, unimportant things to unsuccessful people, but guess what? Successful people do these every day. How small would it be to put one dollar in a jar everyday? At the end of the week, you have seven dollars. At the end of the month, you have $30. At the end of the year you have $365. It's all in remaining disciplined and not expecting immediate results.

The next month, put in two dollars every day. The month after that, three dollars a day. If you do not wish to start with dollars, then start with a penny or a nickel and increase it each month. Simple, small things that will benefit you in the long run. I am sure almost anyone that is reading this book has $30 that they can put in a jar at the end of the month in one lump sum, but that's not what it's about. It's about the simple daily process of physically putting a dollar in a jar. Taking necessary actions every single day that will lead to other simple actions.

What about doing just ten minutes of exercise at minimum each day, or creating a workout routine that you can manage and not skip? What about telling a loved one that you love them every day or greeting everyone that you come in contact with when you walk into a room? Who is the person who makes the difference in success or failure? **YOU ARE**. It's about consistency and not giving up when you feel immediate change is not happening on the time schedule that you prefer.

Knowing how to get out of the comfort zone is not a problem for some people. They know how, they just don't apply it. They simply don't want to work for it. Have you met the person that will attend a conference, watch a motivating film on TV, or even have a friend that will have a life altering conversation with them, and for the next 24 hours they are ready to be on the path to success? After 24 hours, they start to come down off the motivational high and old habits set back in like sitting on the couch watching the latest TV drama. Before they know it, they've watched four episodes and now it's late and time for bed.

Because of the late-night TV show watching, they're tired and sluggish in the morning. Too tired to get up and do the simple little steps that they set for themselves 24 hours ago. Now for the rest of the day they're playing catch up with both mind and body. I am not saying that you can't watch your favorite TV show, but I am saying that you have to change the way you think about these little things. There is a cause and effect on doing (and not doing) the little things every day. Little things are the big things!

IF IT MATTERS TO YOU, YOU WILL TRY TO CHANGE.

If not, then of course you will not change anything. Once you make the decision to change, you must continue to take these small daily actions. A negative thought pattern can cause negative results. It also causes a negative environment and a negative attitude. A positive mindset can cause positive results, a positive environment, and a positive attitude. Have you ever heard that successful people tend to fail their way to the top? They take bits and pieces from each lesson learned and eventually find success. Ultimately, what comes out of the equation is having that "it "factor. You may be saying to yourself, "Who cares?" Or you may say to yourself, "This is what I need!" These simple things can make or break you, believe it or not.

Throughout each day, I take a moment for a deep breath. I close my eyes and take one simple deep breath, letting everything that I am feeling at that time go. Life can get stressful when you compound it: projects, people, family, work, and that inner voice. A simple breath technique that I started to do consciously way back when now happens unconsciously several times a day. What's even cooler is that my wrist watch tells me when it's time to breathe. Sometimes it's right on point. Right when I need it.

At that time, no matter how big of a boulder I carry on my shoulders, I am able to flip the switch in my favor just by taking a deep breath. I simply choose to do it. Not waiting on anything further to happen, or for me to finish whatever I was doing. Just do it. Release the weight that you are feeling. You have to constantly remind yourself that things won't just happen the first few times you try them. Having faith in the process is an important element. You must have faith. Faith is simply accepting the evidence of things not seen.

One thing everyone reading this must realize is that this is not the only way to be successful. Each individual has different motivations and values; no strategy is one size fits all. Despite the minor accomplishments I have had along the way, I still feel like I have a long way to go. There is no time to boost or brag. There is work to be done. Slowing down to analyze and then attacking is the strategy that tends to work for me. I do have some friends who jump quickly to seize an opportunity; they are 100 miles per hour full steam ahead, no looking back. They tend to hit big quickly but it's important to remember that when the elevator goes up, it must come down. It all depends on the approach you take to get to the top. If you take the time to make sure that each floor was suitable for the elevator doors to open while going up, you would have enabled yourself to take only one level down if you indeed fall back. Taking the fast route, you don't enable yourself to have a fall back plan. You go straight to the top and if it fails, you are coming right back down fast. This is what happens to some of us. We see the "right now" instant gratification or the quick bucks and we don't see the longer goals.

Once you make it, you need to have a plan for it. What tends to happen though? People get a big check from somewhere, buy a bunch of stuff instantly, and a month later, they are right back to square one. Successful people do the things that are necessary, whether they like it or not and regardless of their current circumstances.

YOU HAVE EVERYTHING YOU NEED TO BE SUCCESSFUL IN THE PALM OF YOUR HANDS.

Simple as that. What is the difference between

being happy or unhappy? The answers may vary depending on circumstances, but they shouldn't. There is a general answer. Happiness or unhappiness comes from the choices we make every single day. Money will not make an unhappy person happy. Maybe for a moment, but what happens when that money runs out? An unhappy person will still want more, even if they have the money. Being in love will not make an unhappy person happy. They will want more than love once they finally get it. Getting a better job will not make an unhappy person happy; once they get that promotion, they will find something that is wrong with that job and want out. Happy people choose to be happy first and then success follows them. This is why you see people in certain positions and they look like they love what they are doing and exude positive energy. It isn't the position that they are in; it's what they bring to the position.

IT ISN'T THE POSITION THAT THEY ARE IN, IT'S WHAT THEY BRING TO THE POSITION.

Being happy is the first step. If you believe in the law of attraction, then you will understand that you attract the things that you want. Happiness is part of that "it" factor. It's another key component of what separates the great from the good, and allows you to keep climbing the ladder to success.

Would you like to reach your full potential? I know I do. Every day is a learning and growth process. It's a cycle of life. You learn from people you admire, you take the steps in order to apply these teachings to your life, then you share the knowledge with others outside yourself. Not just of how you made it, but all of the failures and lessons learned along the way as well. I read somewhere that all you need to do is add 1% of anything. Add 1% more effort to any skill, knowledge, or effort every day and at the end of the year it would have tripled. Think about that for a second. What is 1% of knowledge per day? Reading one motivational quote. In Chapter 10, this is where you can add to your 1% daily knowledge. What is a 1% increase in effort every day? Reading Chapter 5 and applying some meditative techniques. Everyday simple steps that enable you to generate that "it" factor. If you are not adding, you are subtracting – subtracting the fruit intended to nourish you. If you wish to see change, be the change. There is no pointing the finger at someone else or waiting for someone to push you along the way. Remember, happiness comes first. Take responsibility. You have the power, use it.

How does a person who has the "it" factor handle failures? Failures are part of life. They realize and accept the fact that what matters is how they react and respond to these failures. They have a choice: to add or subtract. Successful ones take responsibility and appreciate the lesson they add. No finger pointing, no self-deprecating actions. They add and make themselves better, simply staying on the upward curve toward growth. Those who stay in that failure moment for long will struggle to learn and grow. Success in one area of your life is contagious to every area of your life. The same with failure. So build, build more, keep building and building. If you failed at something today, start back up today. **DON'T WAIT UNTIL TOMORROW**.

Don't be a small person. If a small problem gets you down or affects you to the point that it ruins your whole mood, you will be limited in the potential you can reach. Any size problem can be viewed as a negative or positive. This perspective depends on the size of person you are. (If you can get out of a large problem, then you are a large person. Don't let negativity draw you in.) It is easy to give up, but equally easy to keep going. You just have to do it. No second guessing. If you see yourself as only what you see in the mirror, then you are content with where you are and do not care to reach beyond the image you see by pouring into your self-development, your personal growth, and your faith.

I'm a planner. I like to write out plans, I like to schedule things out, and I like to write out programs. But planning things out means nothing unless I take action. You can't plan for the curve balls. You can accept that they will come, but if unexpected surprises are something you see in the beginning and you allow it to hinder you from taking action, then you are doing yourself a disservice. Maybe the ball never comes. You will never know unless you step foot on the path. You can't build by simply planning. You have to start building in order to take action to build. Course deviations will require you to use the "it" factor. See it, understand it, accept it, and then get back on course.

Tell yourself, "Today, I will start. I will put my feet in the starting blocks and simply start the race." We are often told to dream big. I say, dream to reach the sky and you will at least reach the stars. It is perfectly ok to dream big. I dream big. The difference is that many people dream so big that they don't really think they can attain that dream. It's an outlandish dream just to have. They say, "If I get this, it would be amazing but I don't really think it will come true." That mindset will not bring any results because of the lack of effort willing to be put in. The successful ones see themselves achieving these dreams. They wholeheartedly believe it will come true. It's a flame that burns from within, mixed with that "it" factor. They understand that it is not an immediate return, but that small every day steps will enable amazing things to happen. What you do when no one is watching means more than the judgments you receive from your peers. If you want to attain that "it" factor, start now. Not tomorrow.

CHAPTER 4:
GREATNESS IS IN YOU

AFFIRMATION:

I am great.
Greatness is within me.

Being great is not a position of knowing it all or being above anyone else. There is no such need to figure everything out all the time. Putting stress on yourself to make something out of nothing or trying to make everything work the way you want is not being great. Allow greatness to flow. Greatness comes with acceptance of being disappointed at times. At any particular moment, you have to realize that whatever happened, happened for a reason and you should take it for what it's worth. Pay attention to the events that reoccur and listen to them. Try not to judge the outcomes, but rather take note. Anytime we are trying to achieve something much greater than ourselves, there will always be a few moments of uncertainty. This is the beauty of living if you see it this way. Greatness is not a superior title or special accolade. It's what's in you and it's up to you to bring it out. We shouldn't be classified by titles or superiority in order to feel a certain way. Have you ever heard the term, "I think boss, therefore I am." Same concept, but being great is not just thinking but also doing. You have to be open minded to the unknown, but this is where frustration creeps in. You tend to accomplish more by trying less. Yes, you read that right: by trying less.

When you try so hard to accomplish something you block everything else out and focus on that one thing. The end is result is blocking the possibility of other blessings to flow through you. To you, being great may be having a lot of money, being famous, or being able to call all the shots in the work place, but that is not what I mean by greatness. You are simply chasing the wrong things and losing your sense of self because of external wants. This is an ego-based desire. If you allow the greatness that is within you to manifest, you will be able to diminish the ego's wants. What are things that dwell within us that we simply choose to avoid? Love, happiness, greatness.

These things do not have to be taught to us. There is no path to love, no path to happiness, no path to greatness. In fact, it is just the opposite. Love *is* the path, happiness *is* the path, greatness *is* the path.

Have you ever been in a situation where you created a goal and accomplished the goal just to make you feel happy? Were you filled with enjoyment once you made it? Probably not, and I'll tell you why. At that moment of wanting to achieve this goal, you put a lot of stress on yourself, a lot of frustration came along, and you started to feel a mood shift from time to time. Once you completed this goal, you felt depleted and just happy that it was finished instead of being joyous of your accomplishment.

You were searching for something external to make you happy instead of being happy that you were working towards this goal. I will say that again. You were searching for something to make you happy instead of being happy doing something you wanted to achieve. Life is bigger than our desires. You have what you need within. Some of us just need a little push in order to wake it up. When you start to over complicate what is simple, it compounds to become a larger struggle and ultimately becomes a harder task to decipher what is real. A lot of this comes from us not listening to ourselves. We should take time to just be quiet and listen to our thoughts sometimes. Do not respond, judge, or act upon them. Just listen. See if the thoughts that arise are of your ego wanting more or less. Can you sit peacefully and clear your mind? What thoughts arise? We are products of a society where we are quick to react to everything and then apologize for our actions later. Taking time to think before we act or speak is a sign of being in tune with our inner self. A simple act. This helps you look past the judgments or preconceived notions that you may impulsively have when speaking out. If you believe you are special, you are correct. But that means everyone else is as well. No one person is above another. I know right now there is someone reading this book saying, "Whatever, I'm different. I know I'm special."

I was there as well before I realized that my ego had a firm hold on my life. You do not need to be labeled "special" in order to be special. Whatever feeling inside you makes you feel alive, that is the feeling that will make your dreams become reality. As I stated before, our ego is never happy. Never content, never satisfied. It always wants more credit, more accolades, more money, and more fame.

IF YOU BELIEVE YOU ARE SPECIAL, YOU ARE CORRECT. BUT THAT MEANS EVERYONE ELSE IS AS WELL.

The problem (well, one of many problems) with letting the ego take you over is that you feel a constant need to strive for something and never arrive to that place. You never feel satisfied. You have no sense of completing anything. One of the best things that happened to me is that through one of my teachers, I was taught to place my thoughts on someone who was less fortunate when I started focusing too much on my successes and losses. Think about that for a second. Say you received a six-figure check after coming from no money at all. Society will tell you to bail out and live your life. But I would say to consider someone not in that position you are in for a second. Someone of less fortunate means. It will humble you and maybe even inspire you to give back. You'll immediately feel alive and a sense of purpose by giving back. I hope so at least.

It's key to stay thankful and appreciative. Let go and let God do His works. Let go of your personal agenda and external demands. Enjoy what you do, but not just because you are seeking little benefits and results. It's key to see the beauty in everyone you meet. Instead of labeling others based on immediate judgments because they look to be different, simply see the beauty in them. Everyone has something in common with you. That something is God. If you let your ego or judgmental thoughts blind you, you will be unable to see God in others. Remember, take a second to be quiet and analyze your thoughts before speaking or acting.

Material items are another thing that tie us to ego. We become attached to possessions and pleasures. The spending money to make us feel good, the nightly glass or two of red wine because you heard someone tell you that it's good for the blood and heart, but deep inside you just really like drinking alcohol. Your personal greatness won't be found in a bottle, in your wallet, from family, or your spouse. It's only found within you. Being in tune with this greatness attracts the right people to flow towards you. Your circle will become different, but it will align with individuals on the same wavelength. You will attract events and opportunities that will align within. All you will be able to say is thank you to God. Thank you for whatever opportunities may reveal themselves. Change the way you look at things. If you came from nowhere, understand and believe that you are now here. Nowhere = Now here.

You're now in a place where you can let your results and accomplishments come naturally while staying away from your ego's desire to feel like the top dog. Whatever is supposed to come your way will indeed come your way. Stop chasing after a title to feel important. When people meet me, I tell them a brief description of the things I have done professionally, but I rarely get into my accomplishments. My description is usually that I played for 13 years, I will give them where I played and that's about it. Who wants to hear about a person tooting their own horn when they first meet you? Even after knowing people for some time, I still do not reveal everything that I've accomplished. I am so very grateful and humbled by everything, but at the same time, I recognize that there's still work to be done and much more growth and development to be had. Every day is a chance to improve at something. If I needed validation from my peers and elders to say that I'm successful, then I'd be like a dog chasing after his tail. Always chasing but never satisfied.

Searching for favor from others will derail you from being in touch with your inner self. If you are indeed aligned, you will trust your vision and your thoughts because you know that they come from a place of awareness. Give up your struggles and begin trusting.

GIVE UP YOUR STRUGGLES AND BEGIN TRUSTING.

What's yours will be yours. Greatness comes with a price. It doesn't happen in a snap of a finger.

Present moment disappointments will arise, but keep in mind that all storms will pass. Some come to clear your path and not to disrupt. It depends on your perspective of things. Don't get caught up in reading some knowledgeable content and then feeling like you know what is best for another person's life. We all walk different paths. It's great to give suggestions and advice as this book does, but feeling like you have all the answers to your own life and the lives of your family and friends is not the solution. If you truly want to help someone, encourage them not by boasting about your accomplishments and how you made it out, but instead by inspiring them to seek and find the greatness that they have inside. When they do find that greatness, be happy for them. There is no need to feel like you should have all the credit for it. Just give them love.

If they feel like you should have the credit, accept it, but know that you only helped them achieve something they already had. Let them know that you didn't do this for a reward in return. You simply want to see everyone win. How would you feel if, after speaking to someone about generalized life situations for a week or so, they told you they need to start charging for their time? Now, this isn't a professional counseling session, but rather someone who feels like they have a bit of knowledge and needs to get paid for it. You would probably stop talking to them. It would feel as if they are fabricated. Fake. Just trying to fatten their pockets. Now, take this same person who has helped you and asked nothing in return. It almost makes you want to do something for them. Who knows if they will accept it, but you want to show your appreciation because they were genuine in helping you reach your inner greatness.

It's important to remember that external desires cannot make you happy. You should change the way you perceive material goods. Remember that materialistic things will not make you happy; you will always want more. Material things are temporary pleasures. These pleasures trick you into thinking that you always need them. You will never be able to have enough. Remember that you don't always have to be right and keep in mind that all storms don't come to damage your place. Trust that it's a situation that will pass and that it arrived to help you clear out unforeseen dangers. Be grateful for the storms in your life.

I AM GREATNESS. GREATNESS IS WITHIN ME.

You are great and you need to become conscious of it. Believe that what you desire from within will arrive. The circumstances that you are in right now do not determine the person that you are. You are not your circumstances. What do I mean by this? As I write this book, we are in a COVID-19 pandemic. Many people have lost their jobs, lost family members, lost friends, and feel like they have lost hope. No one would have imagined something like this would happen for this extended amount of time. We have been unable to get out and see people, visit our favorite restaurants, and many public places are only open in a limited capacity. Many people have lost touch with their faith.

People have allowed these circumstances, as difficult as they are, to knock them off their block, strap them up in an amusement park ride, and press start on the roller coaster. Life has become a bunch of up and down drops, left and right turns, and some upside-down tricks. If you're feeling like you have no control of your inner self and you are now at the mercy of the news stations, TV shows, social media and gossip, you've got to choose to be still. Find that moment to do nothing and look within.

We are responsible for every reaction we choose

to have. Letting go of the worldly traumas will release their control over you and diminish their power. By changing the way that things or people with power over you can affect you, you open up possibilities for growth and development. Once you start to understand the meaning of being great, you will see the world differently. You will start to see that everyone is special, even if they are difficult to deal with. Have you ever wondered why that person who gives a lot, doesn't need acknowledgment, and just pours out love all the time, is so happy with whatever they have? Now you know. You tend to be more attracted to these types of people because without even talking, they pour into you. You feel that energy immediately. They have no need to compare themselves to anyone or seek acceptance for what they are doing. They become less stressed because they know what being stressed feels like and no longer want to be down that long winding road.

What stops a person from committing a crime? The thought of getting caught. What changes a person's mind about getting up and working out every morning to stay in shape? The thought of getting more sleep. We are one thought removed from getting out of a rut or bad situation. We're also one thought away from staying in one! Feeling like dog poop today? Think about a moment when you were laughing hysterically at some random joke and take yourself there. Change your thoughts and the way you look at whatever situation you are in.

YOU ARE ONE THOUGHT AWAY FROM GREATNESS.

All of these situations are meaningless if we don't forgive others for harming us or doing us wrong. Showing love and compassion to both ourselves and others kills the ego and sets us on the path of greatness. Live life with the feeling that you've made an impact in a positive way. If no one sees or gives you credit for what you've done, so be it. Silently praying for individuals when they do not know it has an enormous impact on the energy space around both of you. Know that God is in control of all situations. Visualize that protective grace that surrounds you on a daily basis. Stay the course. Do not be discouraged when you see no immediate change from your efforts. Remember that hard times will pass. Storms are temporary. Do not focus on the finish line, but at the little moments along the journey in order to get there. Enjoy these moments, stay humble, never allow yourself to think that you are better than the next man, love yourself, and love others. I love you.

CHAPTER 5:
A MEDITATIVE STATE OF MIND

AFFIRMATION:

*I will clear my mind of any hatred,
selfishness, jealousy, or anger
embedded within.*

When your mind is clouded by things like self-ishness and hatred, it's easy to lose control of your judgment. A clouded mind does not question if things are as they appear, it simply accepts that these things are as they seem to be. For example, when we first meet someone who seems to be nice, we recognize it and their presence because your mind is in a neutral state. A clouded mind will key in on the person in a lustful or hateful way. We need to be able to observe, make a decision, and apply it without

JARED NEWSON

questioning. If your mind is scattered and all over the place, you have no power. Simple distractions can lead to a pathway of trouble and nonproductivity. When you are not focused, the slightest distraction can steal your attention. You jump from thought to thought and your emotions tend to be pulled in all different directions as well. Whatever your religion, race, or affiliation, meditation improves concentration and helps you to clear your mind. This chapter will identify and explain several techniques to help you along your path.

If you are new to meditation, don't worry – it is not a hard task. Here is a quick seven step tutorial to get you started.

Step 1: Sit down in a chair or against a wall with your back straight to allow the channels of energy to straighten as well.

Step 2: Close your eyes.

Step 3: Take a deep inhale, counting up to ten. Exhale deeply, counting down from ten.

Step 4: Let your breaths flow naturally without intensely pushing them out.

Step 5: Focus your attention on the place in your

body where you feel your breath the most. Example: Your chest, nose, etc.

Step 6: Take five deep breaths while focusing on this place within your body.

Step 7: Open your eyes.

If you were able to complete these seven easy steps, then you are able to continue with the meditation process. What is the meditation process? **SIMPLY ALLOWING WHAT IS**.

Close your eyes in a calm, relaxed position. Place your hands on your lap, your feet flat on the floor and just feel your body. Say, "I will allow what is," four times.

What did you feel? In that moment, did you clear your mind and only focus on the task of saying those words? If you were unable to say these words four times, don't panic. Having scattered thoughts likely contributed to the challenge. Everyone who has meditated has had these scattered thoughts that cause distractions. How do you move past these thoughts? Take your mind back to the object or the words. This may happen several times but eventually you will start to return back to meditation.

Why would I include a chapter about meditation in this book? First off, I am no expert; I only share a few steps that have helped me along the journey. Mental health, physical health, and spiritual growth are a few reasons why I meditate. You can choose whichever reason that you wish for your reason to meditate. If it helps you, then do it. When your mind is calm and focused, you experience life in a different way. You aren't judging, you are allowing everything one moment at a time. There is no right or wrong way to meditate, just do the best you can every time.

Be aware of a few emotions and mind "tricks" that may occur in the beginning of your meditation practice. Anger, embarrassment, frustration, negative thoughts, and scattered thoughts are all normal, common responses. Stay the course. Do not put a lot of pressure on yourself and give up because it is not working immediately. Allow every thought to pass through. Take notice of it all and then release it. Here's how:

1. Notice that you have deviated from your meditation.

2. Relocate the place on your body where your breath is the strongest.

3. Focus your attention on this place.

4. Deeply inhale and release your thoughts on the exhale.

5. Allow what is.

Here is a series of breathing techniques to help remove non-productive channels of energy.

1. Inhale deeply through your right nostril by pressing the left nostril closed with your left thumb. Release the left nostril and press your right nostril with your left middle finger. Exhale through your left nostril. Do this three times.

2. Inhale deeply through your left nostril, press your right nostril closed with your left middle finger. Release the right nostril and press your left nostril closed with your left thumb. Exhale through your right nostril. Do this three times.

3. Inhale deeply through both nostrils, then exhale through both nostrils. Do this for nine breaths. When breathing, concentrate your thoughts on your inhales and exhales. Count up to ten on inhales and down to one on exhales. Focus on your breath.

Some key elements that have helped me be most successful as I was beginning my own meditation journey:

- Wear comfortable clothes.

- Find a quiet place.

- Eliminate as many distractions as possible, such as a cell phone, TV, or family.

- Sit in an upright position.

- Meditate as soon as you wake up (the senses have not yet become fully active, but the train of thought has).

MINDFULNESS

Mindfulness is helpful in focusing your mind on an object during your meditation. By continuously checking in with yourself to see if your mind is on the object, you will instantly notice when your mind is distracted by something else. You will start to notice right away when your mind is about to deviate from your practice, and you will be able to stay on course. Just bring your focus back to that object.

Again, I want to reiterate that I am no meditation guru. I've been meditating now for six years and there are several practices from which I have learned. I will simply share what I do and the steps that I personally use that can also help you. Simple, easy steps. Now, let's meditate.

- Set your watch or timer for 10 minutes.

- Sit in a chair with a solid, straight back and sit erect.

- Close your eyes.

- Take a long deep inhale counting to ten, then exhale counting down from ten.

- Notice all of the sounds around you. Allow everything.

- Give each sound attention. Notice it as a rising or falling sound.

- Return back to your meditation by focusing on your breath.

- Notice all body sensations, aches, or pains.

- Pay attention to which sensation is most dominant and what area of your body is feeling that dominant sensation. View this area as a so-called "anchor point." Recognize it, but do nothing else.

- If other thoughts arise, revert back to your breaths.

- Let your thoughts diminish away, always bringing your attention back to your breaths or your object.

- As thoughts, sounds, and sensations continue to arise, recognize them but do not respond.

- Continue to do this for 10 minutes. Once complete, open your eyes.

I choose to do 10 minutes of meditation daily. For me, it's long enough for me to clear my mind. I started with short two-minute sessions until I became comfortable and began to extend my meditative practice. Meditation is about finding what works for you. Sitting cross legged, laying on your back, sitting with your legs straight; all of these will work. There are many ways to skin a cat, but the end goal is to clear your mind of the chatter.

CHAPTER 6:
EMPOWERMENT

AFFIRMATION:

I am stronger.
I am more confident.

Empowerment is defined as the power given to someone to do something. Let's take a second to think about this. From the day of birth until our last days, we are empowered. Some of us use the power given to us to do only what is required. We have the power to empower others, but are we utilizing this power? The leader whose aim is to empower someone knows who, what, and why they do what they do. They know what their motivation is and who they are inside. They never aim to be anyone but themselves. Here is an example of what I mean by that. Have you ever gone on a blind date with someone and during the initial conversation, shared with them all the characteristics you look for in a significant other? What happened afterward? Did that person coincidentally end up having all the exact characteristics you just explained? Did you wonder whether they would have had all of the characteristics you were searching for if they had starting speaking first? A leader in that situation wouldn't conform to someone else's likes just to win the prize. Are you a person who tries to empower others or are you content just living the life that you live? People are naturally drawn to a leader that pours into the vision of other individuals. Their character always shows up the brightest. Influential character attracts growing individuals. No one wants to be around a person who drains the energy once they walk into a room.

This is the same for leaders. Say a coach has a team meeting with a group of guys and shares a list of qualities he expects the leader or team captain to possess. Nine times out of ten, all those guys will try to act as if they naturally have all these characteristics. Now, don't get me wrong; there are instances where someone may possess all the criteria. If you're truly a leader, a coach will already know the qualities you possess. A man or woman you are interested in will know when you are faking personality traits just to be with them or not. The employees or the company you are part of will know if you are not genuine. They can see the attributes you bring to the table. You are not perfect, nor you should not try to be. You have flaws and should not be afraid to share these flaws. Transparency is a great quality to have. A transparent leader can share their vision and will not have any backlash from their followers. They know that they are under the leadership of someone that can be trusted.

The leader who is not real will eventually expose himself. He can only put on an act for so long. Which do you think is the better compliment: to be trusted or to be loved? Mike, the president of a Fortune 500 company, is loved by so many people in the community. He volunteers at several charity events and frequently accepts guest speaking engagements. Mike's downfall is that even though he is loved, he cannot be trusted because he has a reputation of doing sneaky things behind people's backs. Now you have Dave, who also owns a local business. Dave is not heavily involved in community engagements and keeps to himself. Dave is not particularly loved in the community because people don't know much about him, but the word about Dave is that he can be trusted. He is a man of his word and has never done anything shady to anyone. Mike has garnered all the publicity in the city, but Dave has earned the respect.

Now ask yourself again, which one is more important? Dave has built several lasting relationships because of his trustworthiness. The people led by Dave will continue to follow him, trusting that he will make the best decisions for the company and not just for himself. Leaders like Dave will invest in helping the people around them grow to reach their full potential.

LEADERS DO NOT ONLY LEAD FROM THE TOP.

These leaders are not scared to get their hands dirty and put in the work. It is said that you will not know how to be a commander if you were never a soldier. Would you want to follow someone who is willing to do the dirty work with you, or someone who just tells you what to do yet when you need help, they get someone else to climb in the trenches with you?

I am a basketball skills trainer and coach. When I train, I am often sweating more than my clients. If we are working out at 5:00 AM, I am at the gym at 4:00 AM getting my own workout in before we start. If one of my clients has something specific that they are seeking to improve, such as a bad jump shot or they want to find ways to reach their full potential, I will travel to see their games, have film sessions with them, whatever it takes. I prepare and do the dirty work ahead of time so that all they have to do is arrive at the gym and put in the work. I'm also the General Manager of a $6.5 million dollar fitness facility. I arrive to the gym at 5:00 AM to work out and clean the gym before opening at 6:00 AM. I never bring up what I actually do outside of staff hours because I am not in it for credit or accolades. I'm there because I'm passionate about what we do and I want our team to succeed.

On the days when the gym is closed, I come in to make sure the gym is clean, smelling good, and looking great. As manager it is ultimately my job to get the gym back in order and not point to the finger at anyone else. I motivate and inspire to the best of my ability, but I lead by example. I am not a nagging type of leader. I do not feel as if I should be breathing down someone's back every time they make a mistake. I will say that I am a leader who is willing to get in the mud with you, willing to stand with you, and willing to stand up for you. The staff works hard and they care for each other. The environment that we've built is fantastic and is covered by the Holy Spirit. When we get five star reviews for how clean and well-kept the gym is, I always give myself an internal pat on the back. Not only am I proud to lead a team of people who do their jobs diligently, but I also know that the extra hours I put in to make it a special place are paying off. It's always the small things that matter. A leader's goal should be to achieve success over the long haul. Long term success requires you to have faith in the plan put forward and to execute this plan. Leaders have to implement positive steps forward, maintaining and keeping the faith during adversity.

LEADERS SHOULD NOT ACT LIKE THEY KNOW IT ALL.

Leaders have to be willing to learn and even be mentored. Learn from someone who has seen more than you. Someone who compliments your weaknesses, sharpens your strengths, and holds you accountable.

Accountability is equally as important as being trustworthy when it comes to leadership characteristics. Can you count on your leader to be there? Can you count on them to have your back? Can you count on them to give it to you straight and not water down their message?

Are you approachable? This question was something I had to self-evaluate. I have heard many times that I look too serious or I look intimidating. I found myself purposely putting a fake smile on my face when people came around, which made me feel inauthentic. Like I have a clown face painted on. It didn't feel right. Inside, I knew I was a nice guy and someone who looks for the best in all people. If you did not know me, you wouldn't approach me because you felt intimidated. Being a professional athlete most of my life, it was my goal to be intimidating. I wanted people to fear me when I stepped on the court. I wanted people to know that when they saw me, I was not speaking to them and we were not friends. I am here to bite your head off, not joke around with you.

After years and years of being like this, it started rubbing off on my everyday expressions. Later in my playing days, when I started thinking about life after basketball it was hard for me to balance having an inviting look on my face and keeping up the intimidation factor. How did I fix this? I started speaking first and inviting people to get to know me. If I were to wait for someone to say something to me first, they may not have done so because they didn't know if I would bark at them and curse them out or not.

Towards the end of my playing career if I met someone, I would be the first to stick my hand out and introduce myself. Be the first to share the energy I possess. If people were still judgmental after that, then that was their own issue. I would understand if I was just sitting there looking like I have a bitter beer face on and staring into their souls with no words. This took growth to recognize the things I could control (my expressions) and take action to change them.

LEADERS MUST GROW IN ALL ASPECTS AND FACETS OF LIFE. IT'S ABOUT LEAVING A LEGACY AND CHANGING LIVES.

The impact you have on others is so very important. I remember hearing from a kid once that he doesn't have the right platform to be a leader because he isn't on stage in front of a lot of people and doesn't have a lot of followers on his social media. Let me say this loud for the people in the back: your platform does not matter. Are you in a classroom with other students? Do you play on a team with other players? Do you live in a house with siblings? Do you have co-workers at your job? Do you sit by anyone at your church? You see where I am going. You have the platform, but it is up to you to use the platform that you do have. The right-now platform sets you up for the larger platform later. My platform of talking to teammates over the years led me to doing small speaking engagements, which led me to write this book, which will lead me to touching lives that I would not have imagined. Start small. Just do it. Start speaking and be yourself.

I have a friend that uses a lot of curse words to get his point across. He's a positive influence on a lot of lives, but his dictionary is filled with a lot of four- and five-letter curse words. He doesn't try to be anyone but himself. As a result, he is a well-respected and trustworthy leader, and you know what you will get when you are around him.

When no one is watching, what type of person are you? This is a question only you can answer for yourself. Do you practice what you preach or just speak the way you do in order for people to visualize you as a great person? Leaders understand the impact they have on others' lives.

YOU CAN TELL PEOPLE WHO YOU ARE, BUT THE PERSON THAT YOU SHOW IS THE ONE THAT THEY WILL REMEMBER.

What are the words that come out of your mouth? Your attitude is what reveals your motives. They say talk is cheap. In reality, talk is expensive. The wrong words can cost you a great deal. Are you getting to know the people you are mentoring or did you just read a couple of leadership books and give generalized motivation? Everyone needs to be led differently. Getting to know the people around you impacts the situation in several ways. It lets them know you care. It helps you identify the right leadership approach to take based on the motivations of those you are leading, and it opens the door for trustworthy conversations. Getting to know people enables you to walk next to them instead of in front of them. People aren't looking for handouts. They're looking for guidance. Genuine guidance from someone who's there during both the difficult and joyous times. Now ask yourself: are you a leader? Remember, leadership is all about helping people become the best they can be. The life we live is a learning process.

Every day we are either learning or wasting time. Encouraging the efforts of others, caring, uplifting – all of these are attributes of great leaders. If you can't encourage, you can't lead. You can only be a drill sergeant type of personality for so long. That isn't encouraging; it's demanding. It's totally fine to be a no-excuse type of leader. I consider myself to be one. I feel like you can find a way to achieve whatever you wish to achieve, but I also understand and respect that everyone is not built like that. One of the most challenging hurdles to overcome as a leader is when you pour your energy into someone and they choose not to receive. You may encounter people who are sensitive to anything encouraging you say because they have guilt within themselves and you just trigger the weakness that they embrace. Or they simply may not respond to that leadership style.

So as a leader, what do you do? Do you give up on the person who chooses not to listen to you? Do you give up on the person who thinks that you are talking down to them, when in fact you are just trying to get them out of a rut? Do you give up on the person who is content with the life they have? If your answer was yes, then consider if this person was your spouse or your parent. Does your answer change? Are you going to give up on your mom or dad? Are you going to give up on your husband or wife? Leaders find ways to successfully achieve the planned vision. If there is no vision planned, then giving up is probably the best thing to do and you should not call yourself a leader. Leadership is not just about leading when things are going well. You will face adversity, especially when dealing with people you care about.

IF YOU CAN ENCOURAGE, YOU CAN LEAD.

After that, it's about learning, educating, and applying. You, as a leader, need to empower others.

Pour into them. Maximize their potential. You may not get the credit you deserve; you may not get any credit at all. Be prepared for that. How would you feel if your boss told you to train this new hire so that they can replace you? Be honest. Most would have a problem with that. You may half-heartedly show them the ropes. Maybe be a little snobbish to them. A real leader will embrace the opportunity with open arms. Who's to say your boss isn't having you train them because he plans to promote you to a new position? Being a snob while training someone shows your real character and will shed light to your boss on who you really are. Once again, "You can tell people who you are, but the person that you show is the one that they remember."

Prepare the people you lead for success. Educate and equip them as best as you can. Empower them and develop them into future leaders.

IT'S THE SMALL THINGS THAT MATTER. THE SMALLEST THINGS WE DO HAVE THE BIGGEST IMPACT ON PEOPLE'S LIVES.

CHAPTER 7:

THE BAR IS SET. OR IS IT?

AFFIRMATION:

*I will no longer put a
limit on what I can do.
There are no limits to
what can be achieved.*

Limitations can only be overcome from within. Have you ever caught yourself around a group of peers and felt like you could do more, but refrained from doing so just to be part of the group? Were you nervous to succeed or to achieve more because you didn't want to step on any toes and make your friends feel jealous or envious? When I speak of limitations, I am speaking about limitations within the mind, body, and spirit. It could be as simple as telling someone you are sorry. Do you feel a sense of self-restriction when you do not allow yourself to go beyond your limits? Almost like a prisoner within? Less is more. Think about the time you told someone that they were pushing you to your limit. A self-made limit, that is. A person rubbed you the wrong way, said something you didn't want to hear, or simply gave you bad vibrations. You reacted and made comments that your ego was happy to relay. The feeling of lashing out gave you a sense of superiority. You felt big but in fact, you are small. Your ego was victorious. How about doing less next time?

What is less? Do not respond. When dealing with a person who is pushing you, talking recklessly to you, and giving you bad vibes, just let them be and keep your emotions to yourself. Recognize the flame that they sparked inside of you and allow yourself to feel but not reveal.

By retaliating less and responding less to the negativity, you actually become stronger. More powerful. You take a look within yourself with a conscious effort and do not let your ego win.

ALLOW YOURSELF TO FEEL BUT NOT REVEAL.

An easy way to become less so that you can be more is by meditation. Taking a deep breath and focusing on the space within you lessens your load of thoughts. You are able to be more by becoming less.

Have you ever had someone tell you that success only comes from hard work or good luck? What if I told you that you can't become successful, but you can BE successful? The thought of putting in hard work only to achieve a set level of success is a false narrative. You are working your tail off with the goal at the end of the journey in your mind at all times. While having a goal in mind is good, you're missing out on the now. I am not saying that you should not keep end goals in mind; rather, the steps to get there are the most important elements to focus on in the moment. The end goal comes later. Do you jump up a flight of stairs from the bottom and reach the top without taking any individual steps? Each single step is important. Maintain your focus on one step at a time.

Letting go of your ego, planning, going beyond your limits – these are some of the tasks that you will encounter each step of the way. The end goal depends on the quality of actions taken in each one of the single steps to get there. You get what you put in it. If you shortcut the steps, then you will get short-cut results. Remember, hard work alone is not the key. It requires conscious mental focus and consistent effort to grow into who you truly are. You will lose friends and you will gain stronger relationships with like-minded individuals along the same path. Understand that losing past relationships is not personal. You were both just on different journeys that did not align. There's a quote I have previously mentioned that states, "All storms are not meant to disrupt your life, some are meant to clear your path." Some of the relationships that you lose may hurt you, but their loss is meant to create space for growth. Learn how to be comfortable while being uncomfortable. Growth can be uncomfortable but it enables you to get past your fears. You become creative, you accept change and initiate action. A limit on life has ceased to exist. Is the bar lifted now? Not exactly. What happens when a death in the family occurs? What happens when you lose your job? The natural human instinct is to mourn. You become weakened. Anxiety creeps in, depression creeps in, guilt for becoming more creeps in. You feel like the world is controlling you and you have no sense of control over life.

Not at all. The things that are lost are gained on a stronger level. Accept the fact that staying in a sunken place gets you nowhere. You need to come to peace with whatever holds you back. Create space internally in order to grow.

THE BAR IS SET. OR IS IT?

I love the fact that I can be a voice to both youth and adults through testimonial experience and verbal communication. I am passionate about my job. If I did not love what I was doing, I would not invest the same time and effort that I do. If you are someone who dislikes what you are currently doing, then ask yourself why you continue to do it. If you dread waking up and going to work, then you are doing the life you live a disservice. If you are not alive, then what are you? Dead inside.

I used to be at the point where I needed to buy something in order to feel alive. I needed to spend money on myself or someone else. At that moment, I did actually feel something: a dopamine high. Then I needed to buy something else, and then something else, and the pattern continued. I found myself living for the future, not the present.

It's perfectly fine to go shopping and spend money on whatever you desire, but having that be your only avenue of joy is the downfall. Do not put a limit on your joy. Choose to be happy today, not when that next paycheck comes. Enjoy the things that make you fully present without an agenda for the end goal. I am writing this book because it brings me pure joy, and whatever happens after will be what it is. If you have yet to find that joy, it's because your ego is making excuses not to evolve.

DO NOT PUT A LIMIT ON YOUR JOY. ENJOY THE THINGS THAT MAKE YOU FULLY PRESENT WITHOUT AN AGENDA FOR THE END GOAL.

If you believe in prayer, then ask for it, believe it, receive it, and it's yours. Work hard but do not stress; simply live in the present. The bar is not set. There is no bar. Stress is caused by a sense of failure. Failure is simply how we respond to an event. It does not exist. In the same vein, success does not exist either. It is the same response. Success and failure only exist in the minds of judgment.

Joy belongs to the soul, success and failure belong to the personality. Ask yourself, "What is the difference between how my soul feels and how my personality feels?" If your personality is based on distrust and external views, you only experience discomfort and pain. You become weak. People have a fear of being vulnerable emotionally. If you never address or acknowledge your feelings, you cannot understand what truly triggers you and causes harm to your personality.

Prideful individuals will forgive a person, but will also make it a point to showcase that they forgave them. Broadcasting to everyone how they forgave them and don't care anymore. This is not forgiveness. This is an ego boost for the one who pretended to forgive. Forgiveness does not need to be broadcasted. You do not need a pat on the back for forgiving a person. Forgiveness is genuine. You are releasing the power over yourself and the person you are forgiving. You are no longer handcuffed to the experience you encountered.

Is the bar set? Absolutely not. Accomplishing goals that are set will never be enough if you are pursuing them for external reasons. You are chasing the bag because an entertainer told you how to do it or you decide to pursue a career in gambling because it's fast money. Whichever path or occupation you choose, you will never feel satisfied unless you are aligned with your soul. How will you know if you are doing this? Ask yourself a few questions. Do I feel passionate about what I am doing? Is this gratifying for me? Am I serving myself and others?

Stop gripping the steering wheel so tight and let

go. You cannot control every direction you are intended to go. Let go and let God. Anytime you start to feel negative, acknowledge your feelings, understand that you are not your mind, and let it go. Spreading love receives love. Spreading fear and keeping people at a distance because of a fragile ego only brings negativity in your direction.

Trust allows you to blossom into something bigger. Yes, you have been hurt by trusting someone. Let me rephrase that: your ego has been hurt by trusting someone. It is that and that alone. Your ego. It has nothing to do with you. Trust allows you to be free. To freely laugh and not hold back from having fun. You are no longer choosing to hide your true joyful self. Those days of opening up and exposing that inner freedom are finally here. You are in fact able to experience happiness. It is you who chooses to be the victim, have pity parties, stay angry, bring up past disappointments, and keep your energy vibes low. Choose to be aware of your feelings. Choose to live in the present.

LIFE'S JOURNEY IS NOTHING BUT STONES FOR YOUR PATH. CHOOSE TO STEP UP AND KEEP GOING.

When I was a little kid, the doctors told me that I would never play any sports because of my scoliosis. My mother did not reveal this story to me until I was probably in college. They said because of my age at that time and the degree of curve in my back, that it was basically a wrap for me. The doctors put a limit on my physical life. Or they thought they did. My mother, being the woman that she is, definitely let that information go in one ear and out the other. Being a praying mother (which she is), she kept me active. Kept me in every sport I could think of: soccer, baseball, football, roller hockey, basketball, tennis. I'm sure the ego in her wanted to prove the doctors wrong. As I got older, I became taller and skinnier. I made it a goal of mine to look and feel stronger. I targeted my core a lot because I noticed that I had a slight curve but like I said, I didn't know the story behind it until I was in college. I graduated high school at 6'3" and 180 pounds, soaking wet. Three months after high school, I was 6'5" and 205 pounds, adding 25 pounds of muscle in three summer months. I was on a mission. Something in the back of my head always told me to focus on my core and lower back. All along, I did not know that I was actually doing my body the biggest favor imaginable.

Having a strong core and lower back in my situation helped propel me to last for 13 years as a professional. Having an ailment actually helped me to live in the now.

My daily mission started out as making sure I kept my core strong. Then it evolved into keeping my body strong. Then whatever the next step was that came my way. I am blessed to say that I have always had the ability to focus on the now. When I had my chance with the Dallas Mavericks, I remember one game in veterans camp where I sat the bench until the fourth quarter. Coach Avery Johnson told me to go in and guard Chris Paul full court. In that moment, that was the only thing I thought about. I didn't think of getting crossed over, I didn't think of getting scored on, and I wasn't starstruck. My sole focus was to guard him to the best of my abilities. He actually ended up getting subbed out the next possession so the task wasn't as difficult as it could've been. I'm sure the coach wasn't trying to risk his star player going up against this young energetic kid trying to prove that he's worthy.

I do sometimes wish that I could have taken more pictures and documented several experiences in my past. When I tell you I lived each day for that day and that day alone, it's the truth. This growth started once I left my childhood environment. I was able to see new possibilities and find what I thought my purpose at that time was.

I did not play college basketball or choose the college that I went to because my goal was the get my jersey retired. I evolved each step of the way and the end result was me being one of only four male individuals to have their jersey retired at the University of Tennessee at Martin. Years and years later, I am able to share my knowledge and travel to different camps to help the next generation go past any limit that was placed on them. Athletes have labels or limits placed on them all the time, to include what they pursue in their spare time.

While playing in France, I made two hip-hop albums with French artists and actually hosted concerts, all while leading my team in scoring. It was frowned upon if we lost a game, but celebrated if we won. Making music was a release for me and brought me happiness. I didn't care about whatever limitations others wanted me to stick to. As long as I did my job and represented the organization in a professional manner, everything else was just the opinion of someone who didn't matter. There were no limits. The bar was not set. There are still levels to reach even now. What are those levels? I do not know. All I know is that if I continue to do the things right now that bring me joy and I am giving love to everyone I encounter, whether accepted or not, then what is for me will be.

It hurts me to see parents hold their kids back from reaching levels that they never reached only because they chose not to do anything with their own lives. They're still stuck with a huge ego and now it's affecting their kid. In these situations, all you can do is pray that the parent starts to look within themselves and address the reasons behind the jealousy and envy of their own seed. Clashing with a person like this only makes them stronger. Parents like this love arguing or trying to prove a point. Do not take it personally. Understand it for what it is and do not let it disrupt your energy. Hope for the best, but do not give up on the person.

Whenever you find yourself doubting how far you can go, just remember how far you have come. Remember everything you have faced. Remember the battles you have won. Remember the fears that you have overcome.

I WILL NO LONGER PUT A
LIMIT ON WHAT I CAN DO.
THERE ARE NO LIMITS TO
WHAT CAN BE ACHIEVED.

CHAPTER 8:
WINNING

AFFIRMATION:

Today, I will expect to win because
I have prepared my mind
and body to do so.

Let me start by saying, wanting to always win is not a sign of arrogance. If someone told you to frown everyday instead of smiling, wouldn't that sound crazy? Winning is not something that you have to teach. Facing adversity, rejection, disappointment, and maintaining self-confidence are things that have to be taught. Not giving up on winning is the key. We may get to a point in our lives where we feel like the cards are stacked against us and that we can't win for losing. What if I told you that a loss is a form of winning? Winners have losses. Losing a battle, in whatever fashion, does not mean that particular battle is final. Winning comes in all forms. A high school kid making it home off the bus while passing a rough neighborhood everyday is a win. A girl who was bullied because her parents couldn't afford nice clothes but who ends up receiving clothing donations from her peers is a win. A daughter finally getting an "I love you" from her dying mother while in the hospital is a win. When I speak about winning, I am talking about the things that make you feel a sense of accomplishment. Of course, winning in sports is important to that specific event, but winning in life and emotion trumps it all. A loss is a win because it's a lesson.

You can either accept it or deny it. Accepting the lesson means taking note of who, what and why. Who was involved, what was the outcome, and why did it happen? Which mistake or mistakes did I make and how did I react to the loss then and now? Lessons are put in our path to help us avoid the same results the next time around. Denying the lesson means you are allowing past mistakes and circumstance to prevent you from succeeding in the future. The flame of greatness that flickers inside will slowly die down and will not be allowed to burn bright on the exterior. Wanting to achieve more is not a selfish act. When I was younger, I had hopes and dreams like everyone else. The characteristic about me that always stood out was my willingness to handle whichever goal was in front of me first.

There's an old saying that if you chase two rabbits at a time, both will get away. There's multi-tasking and then there's simply trying to do too much. Through trial and error, I mentally prepared myself on how to approach the plan, achieve the goal and move to the next. By all means, winning doesn't mean you are successful.

SUCCESS DOES NOT MEAN ACHIEVING WHAT SOMEONE ELSE WANTS YOU TO ACHIEVE.

Are all athletes that make it pro successful? Are all CEOs of companies successful? Is a trust fund baby who was left with a lot of money successful?

Success is purely discovering the gifts that God gave you and using them. I played 13 years professional basketball. My last year, I was the leading scorer of a team that went to a championship. I was fully healthy, still in shape, and averaged the most amount of minutes per game in the league at age 33. The next year I decided to quit playing and focus on my family. I could have written a book on all the of negative opinions people had because of my decision. Stupid this, he's making a bad decision that, he's too young to retire, etc. I chose to do what made me happy. I had full belief that God would see me through. Now, three years later, I would make the exact same decision again in order to be around my daughter and see her grow into an intelligent young lady.

WINNING FROM WITHIN.

We are often anxious to improve our circumstances, but hesitant to improve ourselves. Winning is an inside job. We have to switch any negative thoughts in our mind and stack the cards in our favor. How? Do not beat yourself up. Love what you do and do it. Don't hold yourself accountable for results you don't control. Hold yourself accountable for trying your best. If you blame yourself for actions outside of your control, you will sap yourself of the strength needed during times that require you to be strong. Second-guessing actions and thinking you deserve punishment will change your values and determination.

Don't let it happen. I've failed thousands of times. Guess what happened? I tried again, stopped to think, tried again, stopped to think, and tried again. Eventually, I either accomplished what I set out to do or I decided that it was more of a lesson for me to learn. I have a friend that's a tireless worker. Grinding is her forte. Her downfall is that she tries to be perfect in everything she does. She gets tunnel vision and tends to neglect the things that are important to her such as family.

IF WE ARE NOT WILLING TO MAKE CHANGES IN OUR LIVES, WE WILL NOT EVOLVE FROM THE CURRENT PLACE OF BEING.

I've learned that perfectionists are people that try to do things so perfectly that no one else can have anything to say about it. Guess what? Someone will always, I mean always, have something to say about whatever you do. If you were to draw 50 perfect boxes and be labeled the perfect box drawer, would you be happy about your "perfect" title? Maybe. The problem is, that you would lack creativity. Perfectionism lacks creativity. Winning from within requires belief in yourself. How can you possibly begin without believing in yourself first? Trying to achieve perfection distracts us from the overall picture. It's simply not obtainable. Small wins matter. Passing a small quiz leads to passing a big test. Making a free throw in the clutch leads to making a three-pointer to win the game. Asking a girl you like on that first date leads to having the courage to propose to her later. Small wins lead to larger victories.

Learn to celebrate the small wins from within. Winning from the inside requires you to embrace the pressure on the outside. We all know the quotes, "Pressure bursts pipes," "Pressure builds diamonds," "I don't feel pressure." If someone tells you that they never feel pressure, leave from their presence immediately. They are lying to you and themselves. Pressure can be a beautiful thing if you choose to embrace it. There's a better chance of you increasing your strength and resiliency than decreasing life's difficulties. Pressure not embraced will cause the strongest individuals to search for outside answers when they already hold the keys inside themselves. One of the problems in society with winning from within is that it naturally creates self-confidence. In society nowadays, self-confidence is seen as cocky. Being able to say, "I am proud of myself" is frowned upon. Make a list of everything that makes you proud. If that list lights up your heart and puts a smile on your face, then continue with what you are doing. Have a close friend or loved one remind you to take time to appreciate yourself and celebrate the small wins from within. Victory is yours.

Remember that pressure or adversity create the perfect environment for you to grow.

MINDSET OF WINNING.

The affirmation for this chapter is "Today, I will expect to win, because I have prepared my mind and body to do so." What mindset does that put you in?

Even if you have yet to prepare your mind to win the day, saying the affirmation should trigger something in you. If it doesn't, have a friend unroll you because you have in fact turned into a living mummy. Having an open mind and remaining open to new viewpoints can allow you to expand your thought process. You will have the ability to seek better suggestions from peers, which will empower them to feel valued. A winning mindset is not entirely about yourself. Begin your day with a positive pep talk. Focus on the good of yourself and others.

The famous slang now is, "Positive vibes only." Follow it. Remove the negative people from your life if you can. Trying to change a negative person's point of view will distract you from your bigger picture. There is no way of making an unhappy person happy. They will always want more. Focus on what you want, not what you don't want. For example, in the fitness industry when trainers do assessments, the number one reason people give for wanting to join the gym is that they don't want to get fat. Replacing "I don't want to get fat" with "I want to get fit" instead sounds like just semantics, but is actually a huge change. It's about negatives and positives. Saying "I don't want to get fat" sounds like a defeated individual. "I want to get fit" sounds like a person motivated to do what it takes. Change your outlook on how you speak about what you want and what you don't want.

I personally had to change the way I spoke about my goals as well. I would always say that I did not want to NOT have a voice. I later changed that statement to "I will impact every person I come in contact with in a positive way."

WE OFTEN CANNOT DETERMINE WHAT HAPPENS TO US, BUT WE CAN ALWAYS DETERMINE WHAT HAPPENS WITHIN US.

Having a winning mindset is also a form of leadership. There's bad leadership and great leadership; the choice comes from the limitations of your character. Arrogance, selfishness, and reckless leading can put not only yourself, but also the ones following your leadership on a difficult path. The respect that you as a leader must earn requires that your intentions and ethics are without question. It's important to make sure that your words and actions match up. Putting the ones that are following you in an empowered position not only boosts them, but you as well. Only empowered people can reach their potential. Have you ever played on a team and the designated captain was the leading scorer who was chosen by the coach? Their position was not earned but simply given based on level of skill. Leading scorers on a team are not great leaders with winning mindsets all the time. A person whose intention is simply to pad their stats and doesn't care about the outcome of the game causes friction within a team. There are special instances where a very skilled player leads by action instead of words, has a great passion for leading his or her teammates, and is just simply more talented than everyone else on the team.

Their job is to score in order to be in a winning position. Teammates count on him or her to pull them through in the clutch. This is not the same situation as a player selfishly going for their own personal gain. Team members love players who are able to push them to another level. Someone who wants to see them to be successful. They can sense that belief in them, they appreciate the effort to listen and get to know them, and they love a leader who find ways to value them and improve their skills. As a leader, you have to make sure the team evaluates, adjusts, and makes decisions as quickly as possible. It's ok to let people know you need them. No matter how successful you get, how important or accomplished you feel that you are, you do indeed need people. If your attitude is to be served more than to serve, you may be headed down a slippery slope.

EVERYDAY OF MY LIFE, I'M TRYING TO FIND A DIFFERENT WAY TO GET BETTER.

Vision is one of the most important characteristic leaders need to possess in order to win. Vision is the key in order to start the car. Without a key to start, you have a stationary vehicle. I used to always say, "I have no time for anything except grinding and praying." At that moment in my life, I had complete tunnel vision. I was very successful in what I was trying achieve related to basketball. The problem was that anything else that was equally important was blocked.

I didn't make time for any of it; family, friends, girlfriend, etc. I was infatuated with the grind. I still am to a point, but my perspective is different. I am able to do several things with the same focus and also care for my loved ones. It took growth and time management. One task at a time. When one goal was near completion, I would begin a new one.

Your vision needs to be attainable. Whichever vision you choose needs to be reasonable and realistic. The saying, "Impossible is nothing" is cute and all, but come on. There are things in this world that are impossible for you to do. But if you are one who believes in doing the impossible or you'll die trying, then go right ahead. YOLO right? Meditation has always helped with my vision to win. I was never into the deep traditional meditations, but rather the surface level of breathing and clearing my mind. Mantras and affirmations are amazing. Anytime I can sit near a body of water, no matter whether it is, an ocean, sea, lake, or even a swimming pool, and just clear my mind, it's an amazing feeling.

GO TO SLEEP THINKING OF THE THINGS THAT YOU WANT. ONE DAY YOU'LL WAKE UP FEELING LIKE YOU'RE STILL SLEEPING BUT YOU'LL BE LAYING IN YOUR THOUGHTS AND LIVING OUT YOUR VISION.

A vision is just a vision unless you are willing to take the steps in order to win. What are the steps? Seeing, planning, executing, performing, and attaining. I believe the two most overlooked parts of the vision are planning and attaining.

How many times have you jumped into a situation without properly planning or doing your research? How did you do? Some people are naturally gifted and can be thrown into any given situation and perform, but that's not the norm. With proper planning, do you think you could perform better? I'll answer that for you. YES. Now, were you able to attain that level that you think you were great at without planning? Let me give you an example. A fighter steps into the ring on short notice and wins his fight because he's a gifted fighter. Will he be able to attain this level of success every fight just going into the match basically blind and on short notice? I think not. At some point that luck is going to run out and he's getting knocked out. Night night. You should have done your research on your opponent.

Executing and performing are extremely important if your vision is to WIN. Who goes into anything thinking they will lose or not perform well? We all have at some point. Change it now. Want that new job? Prepare for it, visualize it, and believe you will get it. Want to be the person who hits the game winner? Prepare for it, visualize it, and believe it will go in. I hope you see a pattern here. **PREPARE, VISUALIZE, AND BELIEVE**. Let's all have a winning vision.

CHAPTER 9:
BEHIND THE BELIEF

AFFIRMATION:

I am.

I was born September 26, 1984, in Belleville, Illinois, to Jackie Newson. An African American kid that was raised in a single parent household with a hard-working mother. A mother who was raised by her mother to be independent and able to do hard labor as well. Love, perseverance, and work ethic would be the top three characteristics from my mother that would follow me since coming out of the womb. A private kid by nature, I did not have many friends. Growing up, I had to focus on education and housework. My mother saw something in me from the start. I began preschool at an early age and grade school as well. The teachers were against me being young in these classes but everyday at home, my mother and I worked and worked in order to keep up with the older kids. We made sure that I knew everything that the age group was required to know and more.

Going back and forth from Illinois and St. Louis, MO, didn't allow me to get attached to many people except my family members. I had older cousins that I would be around and hang out with if need be, but not someone off the street. When my mother was working, I would be at the babysitter's house in East St. Louis in the John Robinson projects. At the age that I was, I had no clue about project apartments, assisted living, or gang violence. Life was as simple as just wanting to know when the next meal was going to be and whose house I would be going to next. In first grade, I spent time at a Catholic elementary school in Riverview, MO. This was around the time it was still legal to paddle kids for misconduct once second grade began. So halfway through second grade, a situation arose where I was supposed to be paddled. I took the paddle away from the teacher and threw it. They wanted to discipline me further for doing such actions, so instead of fighting with the school, my mother took me out of there. This was all around the time my mother met her first husband, whom I call my dad to this day. A man who stepped up to the plate and handled any responsibility, no matter if I was his biological son or not. To this day, no one can tell me that he's not my real father. It's not about who had you, it's about who helped raise you.

During this time, I attended three different elementary schools in three different areas of Missouri. There was no social media to keep in contact with friends, I didn't have a cell phone and I was not into writing letters. I learned how to be comfortable alone, finding ways to keep myself entertained. Of course, I found kids within the neighborhoods I was in to play with from time to time, but I had a hard time opening up because I knew that I could be moving again. Junior high school was a wakeup call for my mother and myself. I was living around several places where gang violence was routine.

Mornings when we got off the bus and headed into the school building, I would see rival gang members pull kids into the bathrooms and beat them up. In retaliation, the older brothers or family members of those kids would wait in cars after school looking for the people who did it. At any time of day, you could see a brawl happening in the hallways.

During my time as a seventh and eighth grader, I don't think I saw too many days without a fight or confrontation. As a kid, it leaves you on defense mode and makes you aware of your surroundings at all times. That is one thing that St. Louis taught me: survival. In eighth grade, I started to fight often. It was either fight or be called a five-letter word and be picked on. So I chose to be one to prove myself. I was never the one to start anything, but rather I would finish it. As gang cliques started to get bigger within the school, people assumed I was part of one particular group because of the friends that I had. Wearing certain colors would get you attacked walking in the wrong neighborhoods. One evening after school, I ended up having a fight with a guy in the locker room. I got the best of him and his pride wouldn't let that be the end of it. A friend of mine told me that he was going to have his older brothers come up to the school the next day. In my mind, I told myself it was either them or me. I refused to be beaten up and have my face get scarred up, so I came to school with a .22 handgun in my book bag.

Yes. Eighth grade Jared, who had never been in trouble before, went to school with a gun. But let me tell you how God has been with me forever. I was sitting in class and I showed a friend of mine the gun and told him, "I have something for all of them if they think I'm getting jumped." Now, I had never shot a gun, never held a gun, and didn't even know how to load it. It was loaded already with eight bullets in the clip.

I wasn't thinking of any repercussions other than stopping this group of guys from jumping me. While in the classroom showing my friend the gun, someone noticed it. This person anonymously went to the principal's office the next class period to report me. I thank God for whomever that person was. The school day was over and nothing happened. The next day, I had time to sit and think about consequences, so I hid the gun at home and didn't bring it to school. Once I got to school, police were checking my locker. I had to sit in the principal's office until my mother got there. One thing as a black kid, you are more scared about your mother having to call off work and come to the school than you are about the police talking to you. One thing I can say about my mother is that she has always had my back. She asked me if I had a gun, and when I said no, she went off on the principal and everyone else in the office. She believed me because I had never been in trouble before. I didn't tell her the truth until I was probably in college and grown. God had an angel looking out for me that day. The person who reported me was that angel.

Who knows where my life would be if those guys turned up and I did something out of fear. After that school year, I moved back to Illinois to go to high school in Belleville.

Now in a predominantly white school with a small percentage of black students, I went from gang violence to racism. In St. Louis, I wasn't exposed to much racism because black kids were harming each other, so in essence there was no need for racism. Now in Belleville, my eyes started to open up. I realized how sports were political and how the color of your skin enables or doesn't enable you to be entitled to certain things. My older cousin was a senior at the school as I came in my freshman year. He was already a popular person and hung out with the in crowd, so I started school with all of the upperclassman already knowing me. They had a thing called "Freshman Friday" where they would haze all the freshman. No one touched me because they knew my older cousin, so there were perks to it. What I didn't realize is how prejudiced sports were.

I played baseball as a kid. It was my favorite sport growing up. I would like to say that I was pretty good. I pitched and played first base during the AAU seasons. Trying out for the baseball team my freshman year, I saw that there were only two black guys in the whole organization from the 9th - 12th grade. While trying out for the team, the coaches told everyone that the tryouts for the day were over. As I was getting dressed, I saw that I was the only one putting clothes on. I asked someone if we were finished for the day to make sure and he said yes. As I start to leave the locker room, I saw everyone else, still fully dressed, go back to the field. Now I'm dressed in my school clothes and on my way home, so I just keep going. I asked the coach the next day why he said practice was over even though it wasn't, and he said that he never said it.

I asked the other kid who told me that practice was over as well just to confirm what the coach said, and he looked at me like I was lying. So, I left and never tried out for baseball again. I could tell what type of situation this was.

Basketball tryouts came and I was killing it. People in tryouts were praising me for my athleticism and scoring ability. Tryout cuts got posted on the board and I was nowhere to be found. Come to find out that the coaches already had the team picked out from watching the players while in middle school. Coming from St. Louis, I was pretty much the outsider. Wow. Freshman year, I played no sports. That was a first for me, not being on any team in any sport. I took that year to work on my craft. It was then that the light bulb clicked in my head that I would prove any and everyone wrong who doubted me and didn't give me a chance.

During that freshman year we had a few race wars at the school. I lived three miles from the school, so my best friend at the time and I would just walk to and from. One day on our trip from school, a group of white guys in a truck rode past us yelling out racial slurs. They ended up stopping at a corner in our neighborhood with bats and pipes to chase us down. We ended up recognizing one of them out of the bunch. Long story short, that situation ended up getting handled and we didn't have a scratch on us. Fast forward to senior year: I am a wide receiver on the football team and the starting power forward on the basketball team. The start of my senior year on the basketball team, I approach my coach about some colleges to reach out for me; he never did. Guess he didn't care or think I was good enough.

At the end of the regular season, we made it to super sectionals and I had a great game against a school with two D1 signees. This single game got me my only scholarship offer. I received an offer from a junior college in St. Louis, Forest Park Community College. After the high school year was up, I graduated at 6'3" and 180 pounds soaking wet. Two months after, I grew two inches and gained 25 pounds. I stayed in the gym, stayed in the weight room, and used every slander of my ability as motivation. I played in some summer games against pro guys and in one game against Penny Hardaway, I had 25 points. Now people had started to take notice of that kid who was overlooked. I got offered a D1 scholarship from playing in summer basketball leagues. I kept my commitment to Forest Park because I appreciated the fact that they saw a diamond in the rough. I committed to Tennessee-Martin my first semester while at Forest Park because I was a qualifier coming out of high school and because they were the first to be interested in me. The coach that recruited me at Forest Park took a job as an assistant there.

I ended up later picking up interest from The University of Montana, UNLV, and Virginia Tech, but I had already signed. At Tennessee-Martin, where I was later inducted into the Basketball Hall of Fame and one of only four male players to have his jersey retired into the rafters, I graduated cum laude with a bachelor's degree in graphic design. Coach Jason James, who was the assistant at the time, was a man that had a big impact on my college career. Someone who was there when I needed to get work in, someone who cared, and someone who still cares to this day.

He was a coach that recruited me, but later became family. It became bigger than a player/coach relationship.

Basketball, art, music, and fitness have always been my release from the world. Hard times would come and you could find me doing one of the four. I never was a big drinker, big smoker, or big party person. I didn't need to be around a group of people to feel a certain type of way. I would be lying if I said my goal was to be in The UTM Hall of Fame and have my jersey retired. My goal was to make it to the NBA and anything that happened in the meantime was extra. My goal in high school was to make it to the D1 level and I got there – just not the way I imagined. I got there because I didn't quit when my coach didn't give me a fair opportunity. I didn't quit when everyone else on my team was getting looks. I didn't quit when all I had was one scholarship to a junior college. All it takes is one opportunity. After college, I played on the Memphis Grizzlies summer league team in California. This gave me a sense of what the big leagues were about.

I spent my first year as a professional in Germany for the Bayer Giants Leverkusen in the top German Division. That year was a success, for I was an all-star and won the dunk contest. Being in Europe, my first year was an amazing experience. I had never been out the country before and knew little to nothing about anything Germany had to offer.

After that year in Germany, I wanted to take my shot at the NBA but now with the Dallas Mavericks. I played summer league with the team in Las Vegas. My role was pretty limited, but I did compete, play defense, and avoid mistakes. I wanted to guard all of the best players and I made shots when it counted. I ended up earning a veteran's camp invitation from Coach Avery Johnson, who was the head coach at the time. Seeing guys like Dirk Nowitzki, Jason Terry, Josh Howard, and Jason Stackhouse arriving to the gym early to work on their craft was appreciated as a young rookie.

Coach Johnson praised me for my toughness and willingness to learn. In college, I played the small forward and sometimes the power forward positions. I had always been a good shooter and scorer throughout my career. At the NBA level, I needed to transition myself to the shooting guard and sometimes point guard position which required great ball handling. As good a college career as I had, I was not prepared ball handling-wise to win that position in the league. No one worked with me on my handles or ball skills to that degree. I was a three-dribble maximum scorer in college and did not need many dribbles to get where I wanted to go. I lacked the creativity and craftiness with dribbling the basketball because I never had to use it. Being 6'5" in the NBA is not the same as being 6'5" in college. Guarding guys like Gilbert Arenas, Steve Francis, Kevin Durant, and many more enabled me to last and play at a high level for 13 years overseas. Playing in Poland, Australia, Finland, France, Puerto Rico, and Germany has been the experience of a lifetime.

Throughout my playing career, I took an appreciation to physical fitness and health. I had the opportunity to make lasting friendships with many people in each country that I've played in. I wanted to know how the body works in order to gain an edge on the competition. I became a sports performance trainer while also playing the sport I love. As

I mentioned previously, music was one of my releases from the world. It was definitely frowned upon to make music and play ball at that time because coaches and management assumed you were not focused on the task. They did not understand that instead of partying every night and staying up late, I was doing something productive. After playing 13 years, I retired from basketball. I married my wife Cheryl in August of 2019 and decided to be a family man.

My daughter was born in September 2018, and I refused to be a distant father. I waited towards the end of my career in order to have a child for this reason. Some people won't understand your journey and that is not a problem. I was still playing ball at a high level, but giving my daughter all the love she could get and seeing her face everyday was something that I could not pass up. I also did not want my wife to have to go through this parenting process by herself. Years later, I would not change my decision. I know the impact of having a father in your life and not having one as well. My daughter is just like me and everyday she reminds me of why I made that decision to retire from playing overseas.

My joy now comes from seeing these athletes that I train and mentor get better and reach their goals of playing for money. Seeing overweight people drop weight and become more confident or seeing people that I know come out of their shells to have an impact on the world warms my heart. The love is real. As I stated earlier in the book, I don't do things for credit. I do keep in mind the people who act like they no longer know you after making it out of a rut, but I don't judge them. I understand in life that there are givers and takers. If this book has told you one thing, I hope it's that life goes on, but the more time that you dwell on things that do not go your way or focus on the people that act in a way that you don't agree with, the less time you spend working toward achieving your own greatness.

This chapter is titled "Behind The Belief" because no matter how much faith I had, no matter how much I believed, there were steps I needed to take in order to get to the place I am now, and there will be more steps along the way. I had to go beyond believing.

SMALL STEPS MATTER.

Though I am still a work in progress, these 10 chapters are the reason I can look within, love, and forgive the way that I do. I truly wish nothing but success for everyone. I am that guy who wants to see everyone win. There is more to the pages of the life that has been written for me, but explaining everything may have to go into another book. It took a lot of growth for me to even reveal the things I have already said here. But I am at peace and look beyond judgments. I hope someone else has been through the same or even more, and can relate and use it as motivation to keep going.

I HAD TO GO BEYOND BELIEVING.

CHAPTER 10:
DON'T QUOTE ME

This chapter is a list of 100 motivational quotes to read along your journey. 100 quotes for 100 days. Once you read through the quotes, re-read them and see if you get a new motivation the second and third time around.

1. Success is not final, failure is not fatal: It is the courage to continue that counts.

   - Unknown

2. Discipline is the bridge between goals and accomplishment.

   - Jim Rohn (selfmadesuccess.com)

3. One finds limits by pushing them.

   - Herbert Simon (brainyquote.com)

4. The truth is, we all face hardships of some kind, and you never know the struggles a person is

going through. Behind every smile, there's a story of personal struggle.

- Adrienne C. Moore

5. The loudest one in the room is the weakest one in the room.

- Frank Lucas (American Gangster film 2007)

6. They say I dream too big, I say they think too small.

- Unknown

7. Never give up. Great things take time. Be patient.

- Unknown

8. The secret of getting ahead is getting started.

- Mark Twain (brainyquote.com)

9. Never let go of your dreams.

- Unknown

10. Things often get tougher before they get easier. Stay strong, be positive. We all struggle sometimes. Your struggle is part of your story.

- Unknown

11. Try not to become a man of success, rather become a man of value.

> - Albert Einstein (brainyquote.com)

12. Start planning now how to create your own destiny instead of allowing people who don't like you to control your destiny.

> - James Altucher (FB/quotes and sayings)

13. Hardships often prepare ordinary people for an extraordinary destiny.

> - C.S. Lewis (mantraband.com)

14. Life is short, always choose happiness.

> - Unknown

15. Be selective in your battles, sometimes peace is better than being right.

> - Unknown

16. A physician once said, "The best medicine for humans is love." Someone asked, "What if it doesn't work?" He smiled and said, "Increase the dose."

> - Unknown

17. Strength doesn't come from what you can do. It comes from overcoming the things you once thought you couldn't.

> - Rikki Rogers (quotefancy.com)

18. There's a story behind every person. There's a reason why they're the way they are. Think about that before you judge someone.

> - Unknown

19. You were born to win, but to be a winner you must plan to win, prepare to win and expect to win.

> - Zig Ziglar (brainyquote.com)

20. Before enlightenment, chop wood, carry water. After enlightenment chop wood, carry water.

> - Zen koan (quoteHD.com)

21. Faith comes by hearing, and hearing by the word of God.

> - Romans 10:17 (NKJV)

22. There's something you're not hearing that is hindering your harness.

> - Pastor Norman E. Owens Sr.

23. There's always somebody you need to trust be-fore God can trust you with someone who trusts you.

> - Unknown

24. Strength does not come from winning. Your struggles develop your strengths. When you go through hardships and decide not to surrender, that is strength.

> - Arnold Schwarzenegger (brainyquote.com)

25. See yourself as blessed. You will not be blessed if you let the enemy convince you what you did is not good enough.

> - Unknown

26. You will be surprised to know how far you can go past the point where you thought was the end.

> - Unknown

27. If you aren't as close to God as you used to be, who moved?

> - Pastor Norman E. Owens Sr.

28. Good, better, best. Never let it rest until your good is better and your better is best.

> - St. Jerome (brainyquote.com)

29. When I let go of things that were not meant to be, I cleared a path for great stuff to find me.

- Unknown

30. If you really want to get closer to God, learn to be joyful. Nobody wants to be around a miserable person.

- Unknown

31. Why are you trying so hard to fit in when you were born to stand out?

- Ian Wallace (quotefancy.com)

32. Stop resisting life and look at it as a stepping stone to your spiritual journey.

- Unknown

33. A wise man can learn more from a foolish question than a fool can learn from a wise answer.

- Bruce Lee (quotefancy.com)

34. Feed your faith and starve your fear.

- Max Lucado (quotegram.com)

35. Men are anxious to improve their circumstances but are unwilling to improve themselves; they therefore remain bound.

- James Allen (quotefancy.com)

36. A time comes when you need to stop waiting for the man you want to become and start being the man you want to be.

> - Bruce Springsteen (quotefancy.com)

37. I'm coming for everything they said I couldn't have.

> - Unknown

38. Dream so big that you will never reach that dream but the level you reach while working towards that dream will be so great that you will have accomplished much more than you expected.

> - Jared Newson

39. Go to sleep thinking of the things you want. One day when you wake up, it will feel like you're still sleeping for you'll be living in your thoughts.

> - Unknown

40. Your best teacher is your last mistake.

> - Ralph Nader (brainyquote.com)

41. When you get better, those around you benefit. Excellence has the potential to spread in the same way as mediocrity does. If you won't be

better tomorrow than you were today, then what
do you need tomorrow for?

- Unknown

42. When your work speaks for itself, don't inter-
rupt it.

- Henry J. Kaiser (brainyquote.com)

43. I do not believe in failure. It is not failure if you
enjoyed the process.

- Oprah Winfrey (brainyquote.com)

44. There's two types of pain: Useless pain and pain
that makes you stronger. I have no use for useless things.

- Frank Underwood (character from House of
Cards television series)

45. The way you do anything is the way you do everything.

- Tom Waits (quotefancy.com)

46. Lord, thank you for being with me at all times,
even in the times where my eyes may see things
as good or bad, but you see it as doing what's
best for me.

- Jared Newson

47. Whenever you feel like giving up, remember all the people who would love to see you fail.

- Unknown

48. Make your life a masterpiece; imagine no limitations on what you can be, have, or do.

- Brian Tracy (quotefancy.com)

49. Out of the mountain of despair, a stone of hope.

- Martin Luther King Jr. (quotefancy.com)

50. The key to change is to let go of fear.

- Rosanne Cash (quotefancy.com)

51. Just do the best you can. No one can do more than that.

- John Wooden (quotesgram.com)

52. You don't always need a plan. Sometimes you just need to breathe, trust, let go and see what happens.

- Unknown

53. If people are doubting how far you can go, go so far that you can't hear them anymore.

- Michele Ruiz (quotesbook.com)

54. You never fail until you stop trying.

- Albert Einstein (quotefancy.com)

55. Obstacles don't have to stop you. If you run into a wall, don't turn around and give up. Figure out how to climb it. Go through it or work around it.

- Michael Jordan (quotefancy.com)

56. A winner is a dreamer who never gives up.

- Nelson Mandela (quotefancy.com)

57. Don't be the same. Be better.

- Unknown

58. It always seems impossible until it's done.

- Nelson Mandela (quotefancy.com)

59. Ability is what you're capable of doing. Motivation determines what you do. Attitude determines how well you do it.

- Lou Holtz (quotefancy.com)

60. If you never failed, you never tried anything new.

- Unknown

61. Your success and happiness lie in you.

- Helen Keller

62. Challenges are what make life interesting. Overcoming them is what makes life meaningful.

    - Joshua J. Marine

63. Your work is going to fill a large part of your life, and the only way to be truly satisfied is to do what you believe is great work. And the only way to do great work is to love what you do. If you haven't found it yet, keep looking. Don't settle.

    - Steve Jobs

64. A hero is an ordinary individual who finds the strength to persevere and endure in spite of overwhelming obstacles.

    - Christopher Reeve (brainyquote.com)

65. It takes nothing to join the crowd. It takes everything to stand alone.

    - Unknown

66. Obstacles are the cost of greatness.

    - Robin Sharma (treasurequotes.com)

67. Your time is limited, so don't waste it living someone else's life.

    - Steve Jobs (quotefancy.com)

68. Be so good they can't ignore you.

              - Steve Martin (quotefancy.com)

69. You don't have to be great to start, but you have to start to be great.

              - Zig Ziglar (quotefancy.com)

70. Your positive action combined with positive thinking results in success.

              - Shiv Khera (quotefancy.com)

71. Success consists of going from failure to failure without loss of enthusiasm.

              - Winston Churchill

72. Don't let what you cannot do interfere with what you can do.

              - John Wooden

73. Unity is strength... when there is teamwork and collaboration, wonderful things can be achieved.

              - Mattie Stepanek (brainyquote.com)

74. Never forget why you started.

              - Unknown

75. Be yourself, but always your better self.

              - Karl G. Maeser (quotefancy.com)

76. No one is perfect, that's why pencils have erasers.

> - Wolfgang Riebe (quotefancy.com)

77. The greatest glory lies not in never falling, but in rising every time we fall

> - Nelson Mandela (quotefancy.com)

78. You will never change your life until you change something you do daily. The secret of your success is found in your daily routine.

> - John Maxwell (quotefancy.com)

79. Start by doing what's necessary; then do what's possible; and suddenly, you are doing the impossible.

> - Francis Of Assisi (brainyquote.com)

80. Most of the important things in the world have been accomplished by people who have kept on trying when there seemed to be no hope at all.

> - Dale Carnegie (quotefancy.com)

81. It's not about perfect. It's about effort. And when you bring that effort every single day, that's where transformation happens. That's how change occurs.

> - Unknown

82. The most important thing is to try and inspire people so that they can be great in whatever they want to do.

> \- Kobe Bryant (brainyquote.com)

83. Do something great.

> \- Unknown

84. Falling down is an accident; staying down is a choice.

> \- Unknown

85. Work hard in silence, let your success be your noise.

> \- Frank Ocean (quotefancy.com)

86. Life begins at the end of your comfort zone.

> \- Neale Donald Walsch (quotefancy.com)

87. You are what you believe yourself to be.

> \- Paulo Coelho (quotefancy.com)

88. The two most important days in your life are the day you are born and the day you find out why.

> \- Mark Twain (quotefancy.com)

89. Success isn't owned, it's leased. And rent is due every day.

- J.J. Watt (quotefancy.com)

90. When you want to succeed as bad as you want to breathe, then you'll be successful.
   - Eric Thomas (quotefancy.com)

91. Opportunity is missed by most people because it is dressed in overalls and looks like work.
   - Thomas A. Edison (brainyquote.com)

92. Be brave, take risks, nothing can substitute experience.
   - Paulo Coelho (quotefancy.com)

93. It is during our darkest moments that we must focus on the light.
   - Aristotle Onassis (quotefancy.com)

94. Do not pray for an easy life, pray for the strength to endure a difficult one.
   - Bruce Lee (quotefancy.com)

95. Be thankful for what you have; you'll end up having more. If you concentrate on what you don't have, you will never, ever have enough.
   - Oprah Winfrey (myinnerstrengths.com)

96. The pessimist sees difficulty in every opportunity. The optimist sees the opportunity in every difficulty.

        - Winston Churchill (quotefancy.com)

97. The less you respond to negativity, the more peaceful your life becomes.

        - Unknown

98. If you don't go after what you want, you'll never have it. If you don't ask, the answer is always no. If you don't step forward, you're always in the same place.

        - Unknown

99. Without struggle, there can be no progress.

        - Frederick Douglass (quotefancy.com)

100. We all have self-doubt, you don't deny it, but you also don't capitulate to it. You embrace it.

        - Kobe Bryant (graciousquotes.com)

THANK YOU

I would like to say thank you to anyone who bought, shared, donated, or read this book. Thank you to those who supported me without even knowing it. This book is years of growth put into a few pages. I thank my wife and daughter for their love, my mother for her support, my family, my friends, and my friends who became family for their support as well. The content you just read means the world to me. I don't know it all; matter of fact, I know nothing at all. The words that are put together in each chapter are here to only help assist you on your path. If this book has helped open your eyes to start looking within, then I have succeeded. If this book has helped jump-start your goals, then I have succeeded.

Reading this book is the only reward I need in return. I would love to hear your feedback as well. Tell me the success stories and how certain passages hit home for you. I keep this book on me everyday as a reminder to stay the course. *30 Minutes That Can Change Your Life* has actually changed my life, or better yet, the life that chose me. May this book be with you through the temporary storms and the lasting blessings. Once again, Thank You.

ABOUT THE AUTHOR

Jared Newson, born in Belleville, Illinois is a former professional basketball player of 13 years. He is a husband, father, brother and son, and a member of Alpha Phi Alpha Fraternity Incorporated. Jared graduated Cum Laude with a Bachelors Degree in Graphic Design from The University of Tennessee-Martin in 2006. He was inducted into the basketball Hall of Fame in 2014 at Tennessee Martin and had his jersey retired in the rafters February of 2020. Deemed an Ohio Valley Conference Legend in 2018, he played in six different countries, including France, Poland, Australia, Germany, Finland, North America, and Puerto Rico. He also played in the NBA with the Dallas Mavericks in 2007. A big fitness fanatic, Jared holds Certified Personal Training, Sports Nutrition Specialist, TRX, and Strength and Conditioning Specialist certifications. He travels globally to train athletes ranging from grassroots to NBA players. He's held several speaking engagements to discuss the importance of mindset, physical health, and having that "it" factor.

Jared is the founder of the non-profit organization Seat At The Table (seatatthetable.online), whose mission is to reach each seed planted. Seat At The Table aims to empower youth, one life at a time to multiply the harvest for the benefit of humanitarian love. Seat At The Table's vision is to educate, mentor and demonstrate the necessary tools in order to adequately align each kid with the knowledge of all his or her peers. Aiming to alleviate the lack of societal knowledge for all youth, Seat At The Table offers two scholarships per year for a male and female high school student at a local high school in Indiana.

In *30 Minutes That Can Change Your Life*, you will see what it took for Jared to go beyond just believing. Being an underdog and counted out for most of his life, Jared describes himself as a voice for the people who are not being listened to. A believer in faith, guidance, grace, mercy, and a balanced person who loves to be around water, Jared loves spending time with his family and seeing the development of everyone he comes in contact with.

Made in the USA
Middletown, DE
26 July 2021